Winning
Cribbage
Tips

Dan Barlow

Sterling Publishing Co., Inc.
New York

Library of Congress Cataloging-in-Publication Data
Barlow, Dan
  Winning cribbage tips / Dan Barlow.
    p. cm.
  "Official Mensa game book."
  Includes index.
  ISBN 1-4027-1104-2
  1. Cribbage. I. Mensa. II. Title.
GV1295.C9B29 2004
795.41'1—dc22
                        2004005256

Cribbage board on the cover supplied by Pressman Toy Corp.

Editor and Layout: Rodman Pilgrim Neumann

10 9 8 7 6 5 4 3 2 1

Published by Sterling Publishing Co., Inc.
387 Park Avenue South, New York, NY 10016
© 2004 by Dan Barlow
Distributed in Canada by Sterling Publishing
c/o Canadian Manda Group, One Atlantic Avenue, Suite 105
Toronto, Ontario, Canada M6K 3E7
Distributed in Great Britain by Chrysalis Books Group PLC
The Chrysalis Building, Bramley Road, London W10 6SP, England
Distributed in Australia by Capricorn Link (Australia) Pty. Ltd.
P.O. Box 704, Windsor, NSW 2756, Australia

Sterling ISBN 1-4027-1104-2

For June and Al

Contents

EXPERT TIPS

Introduction

For bridge players, there are daily bridge columns in the newspaper. For chess players, there are chess columns. And for Scrabble players there's . . . Jumble, that scrambled word game. Why are these features so popular? Because they take only a few minutes to read. And game players don't want to spend hours poring over textbooks; they want to get back to their games. Which is why, when I was asked to write another cribbage book, I decided it should be organized into a series of cribbage "columns," allowing readers to complete one or two topics a day—or week—at their leisure.

I've arranged the columns so that they become progressively more advanced. I've tried, however, to make the more complex topics accessible to beginners, and to infuse some of the simpler topics with twists that experienced players will find interesting. Beginner or expert, I recommend keeping a deck of cards and a cribbage board handy for easier visualization.

Once you finish reading this book, you will, of course, start winning all of your cribbage games. Wrong! It's not going to happen, and not just because your opponent has also read the book. You'll still lose when your opponent gets better cards and luckier cuts than you do. And you'll also lose—occasionally—because you've adhered to the advice in this book, only to have it backfire. Sorry, it can't be helped, and here's why. I would never advise you to lead the 5 from 3-5-6-9, but if the dealer happens to be holding 6-6-6-7, and you do lead the 5, the play might go:

You	Dealer
5	7 (12)
3 (15-2)	6 (21)
6 (27-3)	6
9 (15-2)	6 (21-1)

7

A six-hole gain! Had you led the 3, 6, or 9, there's an excellent chance that the dealer would have outpegged you, possibly by as many as nine holes:

You	Dealer
9	6 (15-2)
6 (21-2)	6 (27-6)
3 (30-1)	6
5 (11)	7 (18-4)

Obviously, the success of your pegging strategies is highly dependent on the cards your opponent happens to be holding. But that's what makes cribbage so fascinating. If your brilliant plays weren't capable of backfiring game after game, hand after hand, card after card, there'd be no suspense. You'd always win. And you'd never get that tight, burning knot in your stomach, the one you feel whenever you lay down a card, the one that makes life worth living. And cribbage worth playing.

—Dan Barlow

1

Learn to Count the Points in Any Hand

Nowadays there are computer programs and online sites that let you play cribbage any time of day, without inviting an opponent to come into your home and gobble up all your snacks. Sadly, many of these programs and sites do the work of counting your points for you. Thus, when you find yourself seated across the table from a live opponent, you miscount your points. It's like a professional golfer who's suddenly forced to play without a caddy to carry his clubs and provide psychotherapy. He'd be lucky to shoot 90.

There are many reasons you need to be proficient at counting points:

- Some games are lost by just a few holes. And since your opponent usually gets better cards than you do, you can't afford to miss anything to which you're entitled.
- In some circles, a rule known as "muggins" is used. This rule allows your opponent to peg any points you miss, so you'd better know how many you have. And how many he has.
- Even the most patient opponents will become irritated if you take forever to count your points. Especially if you count them three times, and get three different totals.
- Most importantly, if you don't know that 3-3-4-5 is worth more than 3-4-4-5, then when you are dealt 3-3-4-4-5-9, you may decide to save 3-4-4-5. This won't matter if the cut is a 2 or a 6, but if it isn't, it will cost you up to four points. And let's face it: if you regularly make discarding decisions that cost you a "mere" two to four points, by the end of a game you may have lost fifteen or twenty points. You'll need awfully good cards to make up for that kind of handicap.

It's easy enough to find your pairs, runs, and flushes. The tricky points are the three-card and four-card combinations that total 15. Learn to spot them. Here are a few tricky hands to practice on:

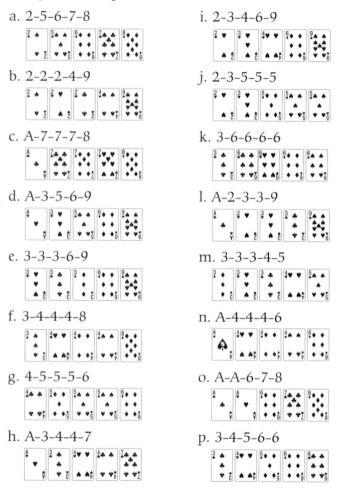

a. 2-5-6-7-8

b. 2-2-2-4-9

c. A-7-7-7-8

d. A-3-5-6-9

e. 3-3-3-6-9

f. 3-4-4-4-8

g. 4-5-5-5-6

h. A-3-4-4-7

i. 2-3-4-6-9

j. 2-3-5-5-5

k. 3-6-6-6-6

l. A-2-3-3-9

m. 3-3-3-4-5

n. A-4-4-4-6

o. A-A-6-7-8

p. 3-4-5-6-6

Solutions

a:10, b:14, c:18, d:6, e:16, f:14, g:23, h:8, i:9, j:14, k:24, l:14, m:21, n:12, o:13, p:16. If you missed any, study them until you see the points you missed. It's essential that you become a point-counting whiz. The game will move more quickly and be more fun—for both players.

2

Put Good Stuff in Your Crib

Even a beginner sees the advantage of tossing a pair or a 15-2 into her own crib. A little help from Opponent will turn those two points into six, and a lucky cut could turn those six into twelve. Here are other tosses that pay off:

1. 5's. Any hand with a 5 in it is sure to be worth at least two points. So if tossing your 5 reduces the value of your hand by only two points, you can probably afford the sacrifice. Holding 2-4-5-8-9-10, the most you can save is five points (5-8-9-10). But if you toss the 5, you still have three points, and you'll often get those two lost points—and more—back in your crib.

2. "Mini-5's." That is, 2-3 or A-4. Like 5's, these tosses guarantee there'll be points in your crib. 2-3 is a great toss, as it works with any low card or any high card.

3. Touching cards. 3-4. 6-7. Two parts of a run. If you provide two thirds of a run, Opponent has to provide only one third. If you can't toss yourself touching cards, cards two apart in rank will do. 2-4. J-K. You hope Opponent (or the cut) fills the inside straight.

4. Jacks. The ten-card that Opponent is least likely to give you is the Jack, because it might get him an extra point for nobs. Does this mean you, also, shouldn't throw a Jack? Not at all. By tossing a Jack (along with a Queen, perhaps) in your own crib, you increase the chances of coming up with a run or even a double run. *Someone's* got to provide the Jack in that J-Q-K run.

5. Low cards. If I listed every card combination that adds up to 15, more than half would include an Ace. 2's and 3's would be well-represented also. The lower the card, the more ways it can combine with other cards to total 15. Aces don't form runs easily, but they more than make up for this fault by turning a lot of 14's into 15's.

3

Guess Your Opponent's Cards

You'd be much more successful in the pegging game if you knew what cards your opponent had, but unless you're psychic, you don't have this information. You can, however, settle for the next-best thing: correctly *guessing* what cards your opponent has. When the play begins, you have nothing to go on other than the fact that there are more 10-cards in the deck than anything else. But once the play is under way, once you've seen one or two or three of Opponent's cards, you can make an educated guess at what else he holds.

"Based on what?" you ask. Based on the assumption that Opponent has attempted to save some points.

If Opponent has no points, it will be nearly impossible to guess his cards—but if he has no points, it won't bother you if he pegs a few holes. It's when Opponent has a good hand that you don't want him adding insult to injury by also pegging an annoying number of points.

If Opponent leads a 3, you might guess that he has a pair of 3's. Or that he has a run that includes a 3 (A-2-3, 3-4-5). Or a face card and a 2. You can't determine anything with certainty, but you can form ideas about his holding, ideas that will evolve as the play progresses.

Suppose you hold 2-6-7-9, and play the 7 on Opponent's lead of a 3. He follows with a Queen. Now you have some information. Opponent has a 3 and a Queen. It would be reasonable to guess that he has a 2. You might guess that he has 2-3-3-Q, 2-3-Q-Q, or A-2-3-Q. True, there are hundreds of possible hands that include a 3 and a Queen, but those that don't involve runs or pairs or 15-2's are bad hands. Opponent wouldn't keep a bad hand if he could help it. So, guessing Opponent has a 2, you avoid playing your 9 on his Queen, as this would make the count 29.

Suppose you are holding 6-7-7-8, the cut is a 10, and the play has proceeded:

Opponent	You
4	8 (12)
3 (15-2)	7 (22)
8 (30-1)	?

You can't guess Opponent's last card precisely, but the cards that would improve his hand (ignoring the cut) are a 2, 3, 4, 5, 7, or 8. Of those cards, the 7 or the 8 would peg on your 7. But none of them would peg on your 6. This is an easy decision. Play the 6. Is it possible you guessed wrong, that Opponent's last card is a 6, and he'll pair you? Yes, but if his card is a 6, he has only two points. Every cloud has a silver lining.

4

Don't Peg Just Because You Can

The most obvious time to resist pegging is when you have enough points to win *without* pegging. Suppose Opponent needs eleven holes to win, and you need eight. You hold 3-3-5-7, and the cut is an 8.

Opponent	You
Q	7 (17)
J (27)	3 (30-1)
K	3 (13)
5 (18)	5 (23-3)

As soon as Opponent led a Queen, you suspected that he might have a 5. You had no need to peg, and you feared that Opponent had almost enough points to go out. Your fears were justified this time—had you taken either opportunity to score 15-2, Opponent would have paired your 5 and won the game with his nine-point hand.

On this next hand, both you and Dealer need sixteen points to win. You save 5-6-6-7, and the cut is . . . a 7! Hallelujah! The play proceeds:

You	Dealer
6	6 (12-2)
6 (18-6)	6 (24-12)
7 (31-2)	4
5 (9)	5 (14-3)

The odds were certainly against Dealer having the fourth 6, and if the cut had been a 10, giving you twelve points, tripling would have been reasonable. But you had your sixteen points, so why take chances?

Runs are a pegging opportunity sometimes wise to ignore.

You	Dealer
8	7 (15-2)
6 (21-3)	5 (26-4)
Go	4 (30-6)
J	3 (13)
7 (20-1)	

Outpegged by eight holes. It would have worked out better to play the Jack on Dealer's 7, breaking up the run, or to pair his 7, if you're willing to risk being tripled.

You	Dealer
7	5! (12)
6 (18-3)	4 (22-4)
2 (24)	3 (27-6)
Go	A (28-8)
J (10-1)	

Oops! Outpegged 18 to 4! Beware of Opponents bearing gifts.

It's okay to form a run if you will be the last to play on it. If Opponent can extend the run, and you can't, it won't go well for you, so if you think that's the situation, get out. Break up the run, and cut your losses.

Is pairing another pegging opportunity to avoid? Many excellent players do avoid pairing, fearing that Opponent will triple. But how often *will* Opponent triple? If the answer is, "One third of the time," then you break even in the long run by pairing. If you think Opponent triples a third of the time, however, you may be experiencing "selective memory." That is, it's easier to remember the few times you got burned two or three hands in a row, than the many times when you didn't get two points because you were too timid to pair.

I shuffled a deck and examined the top twelve cards to see if any card appeared three times—a prerequisite for tripling. Then I repeated the experiment until I'd done it 300 times. Three cards of the same denomination appeared in 111 deals. Nine times, two different cards appeared three times, so there were 120 potential triples dealt. But wait!

1. One fourth of the time, you can expect all three of the key cards to appear in one hand or the other. So there were actually 90 tripling opportunities in 300 deals.

2. And you have to worry about only 45 of them—on the other 45, you're the one with the pair.

3. In many cases, cards which might have contributed to tripling would be tossed to the crib. If you have 2-3-3-4-7-7, and Dealer has 5-7-J-Q-Q-K, the tripling potential of the 7's is lost, as all three get tossed. I would expect one of the key cards to be tossed at least a third of the time. We're down to 30 worrisome hands out of 300!

And not all of those 30 hands will result in tripling. On a few, you'll play the key card first, removing Opponent's tripling threat. On some others, you won't pair the key card when Opponent plays it, because you can score 15-2 instead. Occasionally you'll pair the key card, but the count will be too high for Opponent to triple.

Is it starting to sound like the planets must all be aligned for a triple to come off? If so, keep in mind that a game consists of a lot of hands, with a lot of pairing opportunities. If Opponent, on average, triples only ten percent of the times you pair, that can still be once a game, and occasionally two or three during a lucky streak.

Of course there is at least one good reason for not pairing: pairing is bad for your blood pressure. The time spent waiting to see if Opponent will triple can seem like an eternity. If you find that pairing leaves you on pins and needles, read on. Tip #5 will provide guidelines for reasonably safe pairing.

5

Pair When the Danger Is Least

It's always tempting, when Opponent plays a card you can pair, to take the two points, gambling that she can't triple. After all, with only eight cards in play, what are the odds that three of them are the same denomination? However, since Opponent gets six exasperating, gut-wrenching points for tripling, you may want to put those odds even more heavily in your favor.

A fairly simple idea, and one that's sure to improve your long-term results, is to pair only when you can score additional points *if* Opponent triples. Holding 5-6-7-10, you can afford to pair Opponent's lead of a 7. If she triples, the count will be 21, and you score 31-2 with your 10. True, you've lost two holes, but look what can happen if you *don't* pair the 7: instead, you'll play the 10, and if Opponent pairs that, she gets two points and a Go. You could be three holes down, instead of only two.

Suppose you hold 2-3-4-9. Which of Opponent's possible leads would you pair? Let's look at each one.

- If Opponent leads a 2, you pair, and he triples, the count will be 6. You can score 15-2 with your 9.
- If Opponent leads a 4, you pair, and he triples, the count will be 12. You can score 15-2 with your 3.
- If Opponent leads a 9, you pair, and he triples, the count will be 27. You can score 31-2 with your 4.
- But, if Opponent leads a 3, you pair, and he triples, then the count will be 9. You can't peg, so you're down four holes.

If the worst that can happen when Opponent triples is that you lose two holes, go ahead and pair. After all, you can just as easily lose two holes by *not* pairing—Opponent could pair *you!*

6

Lead from Two Cards that Total 5

This is a strategy based on the likelihood that Dealer has one or more face cards. Lead from your "5-combination," (A-4 or 2-3), and if Dealer plays a ten, you score 15-2.

Holding A-4-K-K, you are tempted to lead a King, hoping Dealer will pair you, and that you can triple for 6 points. But then you notice that the Ace and 4 add up to five. You lead the 4, and if Dealer plays a face card, your Ace scores 15-2. It's always nice, as nondealer, to score first in the pegging.

You	Dealer
4	10 (14)
A (15-2)	K (25)
Go	5 (30-1)
K	10 (20)
K (30-1)	

What if you had led your King instead of your 4?

You	Dealer
K	5 (15-2)
K (25)	Go
4 (29)	
A (30-1)	10
	10 (20-2)
	K (30-1)

Even though Dealer had a King, he didn't pair your King; he played his 5, scoring 15-2 and outpegging you by four holes. Leading the 4, you outpegged him by two holes. A six hole difference! Yes, I could construct hands on which leading the king works out better, but in the end, Opponent is less likely to have a King than some other ten-card, and leading the 4 will pay off more frequently.

7

Answer a "10" Lead with an "11-Combo"

This is a chance for the Dealer to capitalize when Opponent holds face cards. Holding two cards that total 11, play one of them when Opponent leads any 10-card. If Opponent follows with a second 10-card, you score 31-2 with the other half of your "11-combo." Compare these sequences:

A		**B**	
Opponent	**You**	**Opponent**	**You**
Q	9 (19)	Q	8 (18)
K (29-1)	8	K (28)	3 (31-2)
Q (18)	7 (25)	Q	9 (19)
Go	3 (28–1)	J (29-1)	7 (7-1)
J (10-1)			

In hand A, you automatically—and carelessly—play your 9. Opponent outpegs you by one hole. In hand B, you play from your "11-combo" (3-8). This time you win the pegging duel by two holes. A three-hole difference.

Opponent doesn't need four 10-cards; two will do:

C		**D**	
Opponent	**You**	**Opponent**	**You**
Q	7 (17)	10	2 (12)
Q (27)	4 (31-2)	J (22)	9 (31-2)
4	8 (12)	6	9 (15-2)
5 (17)	8 (25–1)	5 (20)	4 (24–1)

It's usually best to play the higher card first from your 11-combo, so Opponent can't score 15-2. However, in hand D you couldn't play the 9 first, for fear of giving up a run. Luckily, Opponent couldn't score 15-2 on your 2, and elected to play a second 10-card, so you still got your 31-2.

8

Don't Always Play Your Highest Card

A relatively obvious pegging strategy is that of playing the highest card possible when the count is approaching 31, thereby increasing the chances of scoring a Go. Suppose you hold 5-8-9-10, and the play has proceeded:

Opponent	You
Q	5 (15-2)
5 (20-2)	?

Your best play at this point is the 10. Opponent can score two points with an Ace, but none with a 2 or a 3. Play the 9, and Opponent scores with a 2 or a pair of Aces. Play the 8, and she scores a Go with any small card. This is common sense. There are, however, exceptions to the "rule" of playing as close to 31 as possible:

1. If it appears likely you can peg more holes by playing a lower card, do it.

Opponent	You
Q	5 (15-2)
Q (25)	?

Your hand is 3-3-4-5. Play the 4, and you'll probably score a Go now and another Go later. Play a 3, and you'll probably score 31 for 4.

Opponent	You
K	5 (15-2)
Q (25)	?

Your hand is 3-4-5-5. If you play your other 5, and your opponent has all face cards, you've lost your chance at a second 15-2.

2. Don't help Opponent to score 31-4.

Opponent	You
K	5 (15-2)
Q (25)	?

Your remaining cards are 2-3-J. With two 3's you can gamble on getting 31-4 yourself. With only one, why risk playing the 3?

3. Don't let Opponent score big all by himself:

Opponent	You
8	Q (18)
6 (24)	?

Your hand is 2-4-5-Q. Play the 5, and Opponent scores big with a pair of Aces. He can do less damage if you play the 4.

4. Trap the card Opponent "apparently" has.

Opponent	You
3	9 (12)
K (22)	?

Your hand is 2-5-6-9. It appears that Opponent might have a 2. If so, you'll be happier if you play the 5, and not the 6, as you may score 31-4.

9

Save Cards That Can Work Together

If you're holding 6-9, and the cut pairs one of those cards, your score increases from two points to six. If you're holding 2-6-7, and the cut pairs one of your cards, your score increases from two points to six. Holding A-2-4-8, if the cut pairs any one of your cards, your score increases from two points to six.

Obviously your chances of improving from two points to six are better if there are four cuts that will do the trick, than if there are only two. Holding A-3-5-6-8-K (Opponent's crib), you can save only two points. Your average score, after the cut, will be highest if you save A-3-5-6, with four cards working together. A-5-6-8, with three working cards (A-6-8), is almost as good. 3-5-6-K, with two working cards (5-K), has a lower average.

Holding 2-4-6-9, you have three cards working together (2-4-9) and two cards working together (6-9). Cut any of them and you improve from four points to at least eight, but because the 9 is working with every card, cutting a 9 improves the hand to ten points.

Of course you can't always save cards that work together, but try to save cards that *can* work together. If you deal yourself 3-3-7-7-K-K, you'll toss a pair into your crib. You could toss the Kings and hope a 5 gets cut for a big payoff in both hands. You could toss the 7's and hope a 2 gets cut, helping your hand, or that a 6, 8, or 9 gets cut, and you have a big crib. You would not toss the 3's, because there's no chance your hand will be worth more than eight points. The Kings and 7's can't work together. Remember, the more cards you have that are working together, or that *can* work together, the more likely you'll get a "lucky" cut.

10

Keep the Cut In Mind When Discarding

Usually you save the cards that add up to the most points. When you don't, it's often because of the crib: you want to put something useful in your crib, or you don't want to put something useful in Opponent's crib.

But the *cut* should also influence your toss. Sometimes it's a sound idea to sacrifice a point, hoping the cut returns that point and more. If you are dealt 2-3-3-6-9-K, and decide you're unwilling to toss 6-9 into Opponent's crib, you'll consider keeping 3-3-6-9, worth six points. But 2-3-3-9, worth only four points, will average more than 3-3-6-9 *after the cut*. You don't need a calculator to see that 3-3-6-9 improves only if the cut is a 3, 6, or 9, while 2-3-3-9 improves if the cut is an Ace, 2, 3, 4, 6, 7, 9, 10, Jack, Queen, or King.

You should also consider the cut's potential to help your hand when you have two different ways of saving the same number of points. Suppose you are dealt 6-7-7-8-9-K. 6-7-7-8 and 7-7-8-9 are each worth twelve points. But will they have the same value after the cut? You'll be glad you saved 7-7-8-9 only if the cut is a 9 or a 10. But 6-7-7-8 is the winner if the cut is an Ace, 2, 5, or 6.

6-6-6-9 is a better holding than 6-6-9-9. Each is worth twelve points, but if the cut is a 3, 6-6-6-9 will be worth eighteen points, while 6-6-9-9 will be worth only fourteen.

4-4-5-6 is a bit more promising than 4-5-6-6. Either is worth a dozen points before the cut, but 4-4-5-6 works out better if the cut is an Ace, 2, 6 or 7. 4-5-6-6 works out better only if the cut is a 3, 4, or 9. Don't neglect those opportunities to pick up additional points.

11

Lead from Three Cards That Total 16

Here's another strategy based on the possibility that Dealer has saved face cards, but this time we're expecting him to have one or two 5's with his 10's.

Holding A-6-8-9, you note that the A, 6, and 9 add up to 16. You lead the 6, and Dealer plays a queen. So far, so good. Now you play the 9, making the count 25. If Luck is with you, Dealer will play a 5, and your ace will score 31-2.

You	Dealer
6	Q (16)
9 (25)	5 (30)
A (31-2)	J
8 (18)	5 (23-1)

Note that it would have been a mistake to play the Ace any earlier. Why? Because you must put the count above 21 with your second card in order to force Dealer to play his 5. If you play the ace first—or second—Dealer can play two face cards, and you won't score 31-2.

Two of the sweeter "16-combinations" are 3-4-9 and 4-6-6. Holding 3-4-9, start with the 9. Holding 4-6-6, save the 4 for last. If Dealer has face cards and 5's, there's a good chance you'll score 31-5!

You	Dealer	You	Dealer
6	J (16)	9	K (19)
6 (22)	5 (27)	3 (22)	5 (27)
4 (31-5)	Q	4 (31-5)	Q
6 (15-2)	K (25–1)	8 (18)	5 (23-1)

Obviously Dealer won't have faces and 5's whenever you want him to, but when he does have them, he usually has a pretty good hand, so it's only fair that you make him pay dearly for holding those nice cards.

12

Assume Dealer Will Peg on Your Lead

If you could see through the backs of Dealer's cards, he'd almost never peg on your opening lead. But with no idea what he's holding, it's a good idea to assume Dealer will peg on whichever card you lead. Once you've made this assumption, lead the card that allows you to regain the points Dealer scores.

The most obvious way to set yourself up for "counter-pegging" is to lead from a pair, hoping Dealer will pair your lead, allowing you to triple his pegging points. Dealers don't always pair your lead when they can, fearing you'll pick up six big holes, but it's certainly better to lead from your pair and have Dealer decide not to pair you, than to lead one of your other cards, only to have Dealer annoyingly pair *that* one.

You can also set yourself up by leading from a 15-2 combination. Lead the 10 from 5-10, and if Dealer scores 15-2, you pair his 5. This works with the 6-9 combination, as well as the 7-8.

- From 6-9, you'll want to lead the 6. If Dealer scores 15-2, you pair his 9, with no worries that he'll triple. If you start with the 9, and he scores 15-2, he could triple your 6 if you pair.
- From 7-8, you'll want to lead the 8. This time tripling is a worry no matter which card you start with, but if Dealer triples your 8, he also scores 31-2:

You	Dealer	You	Dealer
8	7 (15-2)	7	8 (15-2)
7 (22-2)	7 (29-6)	8 (23-2)	8 (31-8)

A final means of setting up counter-pegging is to lead a card which, if paired, allows you to score 15-2. Holding both a 4 and a 7, lead the 4; if it's paired, you score 15-2 with your 7. Similarly, lead a 3 when holding a 9, lead a 6 when holding a 3, and lead a 7 when holding an ace. In each case, you score 15-2 if Dealer pairs your lead.

It's not uncommon for Dealer to strike first in the pegging, but if you are ready with your counter-strike, he won't be leaving you in his dust.

13

Use the Count

If you can't score points, or set yourself up for future pegging, your play might be influenced by the count. If you
put the count in the 0 to 4 range, Opponent can't score
15-2. If you put the count in the 16-20 range, Opponent
can't score 31-2. These are fairly obvious ways of using
the count to your advantage. Here are two others:

1. Having no idea what Opponent has, you can still give
   him every opportunity to help you snag an extra point
   or two.

You	Dealer
9	K (19)
?	

   If your remaining cards are A-8-10, play the 10, making the count 29. You are hoping Dealer will have to play
an Ace, allowing you to score 31-4. You never know—he
could have A-J-Q-K.

   If your remaining cards are 2-8-10, you would play the
8, making the count 27, hoping Dealer will have to play a
2. If there's a chance Opponent will play a card you can
pair, you may as well arrange for the count to be in your
favor when he does so.

2. It can be irritating to your opponent if you make the
   count 11. He won't want to make the count 21, and if
   he's holding one or more 10-cards, you've limited his
   choices. You may even catch him napping, leading his
   only non-10.

A		**B**	
Opponent	**You**	**Opponent**	**You**
9	2 (11)	3	8 (11)
Q (21)	Q (31-4)	2 (13)	2 (15-4)
10	3 (13)	10 (25)	5 (30-1)
J (23)	4 (27–1)	J	5 (15-3)

In Hand A, Opponent left himself with nothing but 10-cards, which quickly proved embarrassing. In Hand B, Opponent was forced to decide whether your 8 was accompanied by at least one 10-card (8-9-10-J, for instance), or whether playing his 2 would give up 15-4. He guessed wrong.

BONUS TIP

Don't make the count 11 if doing so might discourage Opponent from helping you score. Suppose you hold 2-3-K-K, and Opponent leads a 9. If you play the 2, making the count 11, Opponent, holding 9-9-10-J, will be reluctant to play a 10-card, which, in this case, is what you want him to do. Play a King on Opponent's 9, and he's more likely to help you score 31-2.

14

Lead from Three Cards That Total 11

Here is another strategy based on the strong possibility that Dealer has saved several face cards. By leading from your "11-combination," you hope to score 31-2. Here are two examples.

In Hand A, holding 2-2-6-7, you notice that 2, 2, and 7 add up to 11. You lead one of them, and if Dealer plays a face card, play a second card from your 11-combination (not the 6!). If Dealer now plays a second face card, you score 31-2.

A		**B**	
You	**Dealer**	**You**	**Dealer**
2	K (12)	7	J (17)
7 (19)	Q (29)	3 (20)	J (30)
2 (31-2)	J	A (31-2)	Q
6 (16)	5 (21–1)	8 (18)	5 (23-1)

In Hand B, holding A-3-7-8, you realized immediately that A-3-7 adds up to 11. So you didn't play the 8. You kept playing from your 11-combination for as long as Dealer played 10's.

Note that your second card in each sequence above prevented Dealer from playing his 5 without offering you a run. If Dealer has all 10's, great. If he has something else with his 10's, the 11-combination still works, as long as he keeps playing 10's.

Perhaps the best 11-combinations for non-dealer are 2-3-6 and A-4-6. These allow you to lead low and score 15-2 if Dealer plays a 10, and to score 31-2 if Dealer plays a second 10. You'll often save two tens when you have 2-3 or A-4, but if you have a chance, save a 6. You may score the first four pegging holes—not bad for a non-dealer.

15

Assume Opponent Can Peg on Any Card You Play

We've seen how the opening lead can be chosen with an eye toward counter-pegging. This strategy may be used further on in the play. Suppose Opponent leads a King and you are holding 2-3-9-10. If you play the 10 and Opponent pairs it, he gets two points and a Go. If you play the 9 and Opponent pairs it, the count is 28; your 3 scores 31-2.

Had your hand been A-4-9-10, playing the 10 on Opponent's King would assure equal counter-pegging; should Opponent pair the 10, your Ace scores 31-2.

Here's a hand where both players employ this strategy:

Opponent	You
4	K (14)
6 (20)	3 (23)
7 (30-1)	7
5 (12)	5 (17-3)

- Opponent leads a 4, knowing that if you pair it, he can score 15-2 with his 7.
- You play your King, knowing that if Opponent pairs it, you can score 31-2 with your 7.
- Opponent plays his 6, knowing that if you pair it, he can score 31-2 with his 5.
- You play your 3, knowing that if Opponent pairs it, you can score 31-2 with your 5.
- Note that Opponent could have safely played his 5 on your King. If you pair the 5, his 7 provides protection, scoring 31-2.

If you can't peg, and you have more than one safe choice, choose the one for which you have an answer to Opponent's pegging.

16

Don't Toss Cards
That Total 10 into Your Crib

First the exception to the rule: 5-5. Toss yourself two 5's anytime you can spare them. Now, then . . .

If you can't throw actual points into your own crib, you try to throw two cards that can work together with a third card. Why? Because if three cards in your crib are working together, it's more likely the fourth or fifth card will be helpful. If you toss 8-10, you need a 9 to get all of your cards working. If you toss 3-Q you need a 2. If you toss 2-6 you need a 7. You have three chances to get the card you need: the cut, and Opponent's toss. If two of those three chances pan out, your crib improves to six or eight points.

This is all well and good, but if the card that gets all of your other cards working is a 5, you can pretty well assume that your opponent won't be donating it to your cause, and that you'll have to rely on the cut. In other words, if you need a 5 to "complete" your crib, your chances of getting it aren't nearly as good as they are if you need some other card. Which is why tossing A-9, 2-8, 3-7, or 4-6 into your own crib seldom pays off with big points. It's not the end of the world if you must make one of these tosses, but unless the cut is a 5, you'll probably need both of Opponent's tossed cards and the cut to work for you if you want a nice 10 or 12 point crib—a tall order.

Obviously, there will be times when your other four cards go together, and you must toss yourself 2-8. But when you do have a choice, lean away from tosses that total 10.

When it's not your crib, you're often better off tossing cards that do total 10. From A-2-9-K-K-K, toss A-9, but from A-2-8-K-K-K, toss 2-8. True, Dealer will not be disinclined to toss a 5 in his own crib, but more often than not, Dealer's 5 is so useful in his hand, he holds onto it.

17

Note the Cards Opponent Doesn't Have

We saw the advantage, in Tip #3, of guessing Opponent's cards. But guesswork is guesswork—sometimes you guess wrong. If Opponent has two Aces and a Jack showing, you'll reasonably guess that he is more likely to have a 4 than a 9. If you thus play your 9 instead of your 4, and he pairs you, well, that's cribbage.

There is a strategy closely related to guessing Opponent's cards, however, that does not involve mere chance. To illustrate, imagine that you hold 3-8-9-10. You lead the 10. Opponent plays a King, you play the 8 for 28, and he plays a deuce: 30 and a Go. Now you must play your 9 or your 3. You note that Opponent has played a King and a deuce. Because a 3 would be a logical accompaniment to those cards, you start to play your 9. But wait! If Dealer had a 3, he would have played it when the count was 28. So your safest play is the 3, which pays off, as Dealer's remaining cards turn out to be 6-7.

Even more revealing than Opponent's failure to score 15-2's, pairs, and runs, is his failure to play any card at all. If he says, "Go," when the count is at 27, he's guaranteed to have nothing lower than a 5. If he says, "Go," when the count is at 22, he's guaranteed to have nothing lower than a 10! Here are two sample hands:

You	Dealer
4	K (14)
9 (23)	Go
?	

Your last two cards are a 4 and a 5. Knowing Dealer has nothing lower than a 9, and that there's an excellent chance he's about to play a 10-card, you naturally play the 4, and later score 15-2 with your 5.

Opponent	You
6	9 (15-2)
5 (20)	8 (28-1)
4	?

Your last two cards are 7-9. You realize that if you play the 7, Opponent can pair your 7, or score 15-2 with another 4. If you play the 9, he can pair your 9, or score 15-2 with a 2. But wait! He can't have a 2, as he was unable to play when the count was 28. And if he has a 9, why didn't he pair your first 9? The 9 is perfectly safe.

Anytime your Opponent says, "Go," or fails—without reason—to score points, make a mental note of the card or cards he doesn't have. Once you've figured out what he *doesn't* have, it'll be easier to guess what he *does* have.

18

Needing Two Holes, Save a Diversity of Cards

You're two holes from victory. Opponent needs seven holes. She leads out with a 3. You glance at your hand and discover that you've saved 7-7-8-8. As the play proceeds, you mentally will Opponent to make the count 23 or 24, but she never does.

Opponent	You
3	8 (11)
4 (15-2)	7 (22)
6 (28-1)	7
5 (12)	8 (20-1)

I didn't mention which cards you tossed in your crib, but a 3 would have pegged on Opponent's opening lead, a 4 would have pegged on her 4, an Ace or a 2 would have gotten you a Go, with another Go still to come, and a 5 or a 6 would have pegged on Opponent's 5. If you threw away any card lower than a 7, you could have won this game.

When you need two holes, don't save your points; save a diversity of cards. If you save 3-6-6-9, you can peg if Opponent leads a 3, a 6, or a 9. Better to toss 6-9 in your crib, and save 2-3-6-7. You can still peg on the lead of a 3, 6, or 9, but now you can also peg on a 2, 7, or 8.

This strategy applies as well when you're *not* Dealer—if Dealer is also close to home. If both of you need two holes, and you tossed 2-7, keeping 2-3-4-7, lead a 2. You *could* lose immediately, but if you are lucky enough to survive your opening lead, you can peg out if Dealer plays, on your 2, an Ace, 3, 4, 6, 7, 9, 10, J, Q, or K. Had you tossed 3-4, keeping 2-2-7-7, and led a 2, you'd have pegged out only if Dealer played a 6 or a 7. By saving a diversity of cards, you give yourself more chances to peg the two holes you need.

19

Don't Keep Playing Tens

Your opponent may not have read this book. She may never have read any book about cribbage. She may never have *played* cribbage. But a good many cribbage strategies require only some good old-fashioned card sense, so when your opponent plays a card, assume she had a reason for playing it.

We've seen several strategies that rely on Opponent having face cards and 10's. You can expect your opponent to be familiar with these strategies as well. And obviously if your opponent is employing strategies based on your playing 10-cards, it must be to your advantage to avoid doing so.

If Opponent leads a low card, she's often hoping you'll play a 10 so that she can score 15-2 with her other low card. Can you avoid doing so?

If Opponent leads from three cards that total 11, she wants you to play two 10's. Is there something else you can safely play?

If Opponent leads from three cards that total 16, she wants you to play a 10 and a 5. Do you have another choice?

If you lead a 10-card, Opponent may play from two cards that total 11, hoping you'll play another 10-card. Can you play something else?

Sometimes, of course, the answer will be No; you'll have all tens or all tens and 5's. Or your other choices look too dangerous. If that's the case, you're stuck. But some players with only two 10-cards will automatically play them at the first opportunity. Don't be one of those players.

20

If Dealer Needs Two Holes, Play the Odds

Occasionally you'll find yourself involved in a pegging duel, with the Dealer needing only two holes to win. It will probably do little good to try and guess his cards, as he had no reason to save a good hand. More likely he saved a diversity of cards, enabling him to peg on several of your potential leads.

In such a situation you should consistently play the card he is least likely to peg on. On opening lead, that will almost always be a low card, preventing Dealer from scoring 15-2. Dealer knows a low card is your best lead, of course, and will probably save low cards in hopes of pairing your lead. Does this mean you should lead a high card? No, you should lead low, gambling that he wasn't dealt the same low card you are leading. Lead a high card, and Dealer can pair or score 15-2.

Here's a pegging sequence in which both players are two holes from victory (the cut is a 5):

You	Dealer
3	6 (9)
3 (12)	7 (19)
A (20)	5 (25)
4 (29-1)	9 (9-1)

- Holding two 3's, you know that the 3 is the card Dealer is least likely to pair.
- He doesn't pair, but by playing a 6, he limits your pegging chances—you can peg only with a 6.
- Your next play is the safe 3—you already know he has no 3, so he can't pair or score 15-2.
- His 7 ensures that you can peg only with a 7 of your

own (his 5 or his 9 would have given you more than one pegging card).

- Your Ace restricts his chances as well (the 4 would have let him peg with a 4 or an 8).
- With a 5 in his hand and a 5 as the cut, and knowing you have no 6, Dealer makes the count 25 with his 5 (his 9 would have let you peg with a 2, of which there are four available).
- Luckily, Dealer's last card is not a 2, and you get to count your hand. Whew!

21

Give Yourself a Chance

Sometimes Dealer is so close to home, it's unreasonable to hope he won't go out with his pegging, his two hands, and first count next hand. In such cases, you must hope to go out first. Of course, you won't go out first if you don't save cards that give you a chance of doing so.

Suppose you need twenty-five holes to win, and Dealer needs five. You pick up 4-4-6-6-9-9. Early in the game you would save 6-6-9-9. But the most you can score with 6-6-9-9 is twenty points. You need twenty-five. Even if you get a cut (6 or 9), you'll still need to peg five holes, while keeping Dealer from pegging five. Your chances are better if you save 4-4-6-6. That's only four points, but if you cut a 5, you'll have to peg only one hole.

Let's look at two more examples:

1. Holding 3-3-3-6-7-Q, needing eight points to avoid a loss, you would save 3-3-3-6, of course. You already have eight points. But what if you need twelve points? If you save 3-3-3-6, you'll need to cut a 3, 6, or 9. There are four 9's, three 6's, and one 3 available to cut. A total of eight winning cuts. If you save 3-3-3-7, you'll get twelve points if you cut a 2, 3, 5, or 9. There are thirteen winning cuts available.

2. Suppose you need twelve points to go out, and Dealer needs seven. Which cards do you save from 2-3-4-9-10-J? To get twelve points, you must save 2-3-4 and one other card. It's tempting to make the Jack your fourth card, in case it's nobs, but if you save the Jack, only a 2 or 3 cut will give you the points you need. If you save the 9, you get twelve points if you cut a 2, 3, or 4. There's no guarantee you'll peg anything, so keep the cards most likely to get you the points you need.

The principle of keeping the cards that give you a chance can apply in the pegging game as well. The following hand was made all the more spectacular by the fact that I happened to need exactly nine holes when it was played, while my opponent needed four, and had first count. I dealt myself 3-6-10-K-K-K, and saved 10-K-K-K. The play proceeded:

Opponent	Me
3	10 (13)
J (23)	Go
3 (26)	
5 (31-2)	K
	K (20-2)
	K (30-7)

Earlier in the game I'd have saved 3-K-K-K, in case the cut were a 2, but with Opponent highly likely to have enough points, I saved the 10, improving the chances the count would get over 21 while I still had all three Kings. My one regret was that the game was played online, so I didn't get to enjoy the stunned look on Opponent's face.

BONUS TIP

It's a good idea, when holding three of a kind as Dealer, to play your other card first:

Opponent	You
10	8 (18)
10 (28)	A (29)
Go	A (30-2)
	A (31-8)
Q	
5 (15-3)	

It's tempting to play an Ace on Opponent's first 10, as he might have a 9, but even if he has a 9, his pegging won't match yours if you get to play your Aces consecutively. Ten holes pegged is like an extra hand.

22

Expect Opponent to Have a 5

Naturally, you would prefer that your opponent never have any 5's, but he seems to get more than his share. And let's face it, he's not throwing a 5 into your crib, not if he can help it. He'll gladly sacrifice a few points to keep that 5 away from you, even if the 5 is worthless in his own hand.

Another thing about your opponent: he's scored so many 15-2's with his 5's over the years, he'll often hang onto a 5 until the bitter end, hoping the count will revert to 0, and you'll play a 10-card. Well, you can take advantage of this tendency if you happen to have 3-4, 4-6, or 6-7.

A		**B**	
Opponent	**You**	**Opponent**	**You**
Q	8 (18)	Q	6 (16)
J (28)	2 (30-1)	Q (26)	3! (29-1)
K	7 (17)	Q	6 (16)
5 (22)	6 (28–4)	5 (21)	4 (25-4)

In Hand A, Opponent could have jettisoned his 5 on your 8, or led it when the count got back to 0, but he didn't. His loss is your gain. Of course, you had to do your part by hanging onto the 6 and 7. If you had played one of them on his Queen, you could not have punished him for holding onto his 5. In Hand B, playing the 3 was a bit risky. Opponent could have been holding Q-Q-A-A. But she had the cards you were hoping she did.

Is a 5 the only card you can trap this way? No, you can trap any card. But a 5 is the card Opponent is least likely to toss in your crib, and it's a card she's reluctant to part with, so the last card in her hand will frequently be a 5.

23

Dump That 5!

After Tip #22, you knew this was coming. If Opponent is trying to trap your 5 into a run, you should be trying to get the 5 out of your hand while the getting's good.

You	Dealer
K	10 (20)
Q (30-1)	2
J (12)	3 (15-2)
5 (20)	4 (24-4)

You could have dumped the 5 on Dealer's 10, or on his 2. It was reasonable not to dump it on the 10—you were hoping he'd lead another 10. But once he led the 2, the 5 became a liability. Just because your opponent knows how to trap your 5, you don't have to let him do it.

There's a second good reason to dump your 5 early: you may end up leading it with the count at 0.

A		**B**	
You	**Dealer**	**You**	**Dealer**
Q	9 (19)	K	10 (20)
Q (29-1)	9	K (30)	A (31-2)
K (19)	10 (29-1)	5	10 (15-2)
5	J (15-3)	5 (20)	4 (24-1)

In Hand A, had you dumped the 5 on either of Dealer's 9's, you'd have saved a few points.

In Hand B, with two 5's, there's just no excuse for not dumping one of them on Dealer's first 10.

Should Dealer dump his 5 as well? Actually, if Dealer doesn't have two cards with which to trap Opponent's 5, he may be better off *not* dumping his own 5. Since Dealer most often gets last card, holding a 5 frequently allows him to pair Opponent's 5, or to score 15-2.

24

Play Your Least Useful Card Early

You'd like all your cards to be working, scoring points, but you won't be that lucky. Often you'll save a hand in which three cards are working, but not the fourth. Even a nice hand, like 5-5-8-8-8-Q (your crib), will force you to save three working cards and one "odd man out." On such occasions, it's a good idea to play your non-working card early.

Just as you are trying to guess your opponent's remaining cards, she is trying to guess yours. Suppose you hold 2-6-7-K. If the first two cards you play are the 2 and the 7, Opponent may correctly guess that you have a 6. If the first two cards you play are the 2 and the King, Opponent may incorrectly guess that you have a 3. Certainly it's to your advantage to keep her in the dark about your holding. Contrast these hands:

A		**B**	
You	**Dealer**	**You**	**Dealer**
4	J (14)	4	J (14)
Q (24)	3 (27)	8 (22)	5 (27)
3 (30-3)	6	3 (30-1)	6
8 (14)	5 (19-1)	Q (16)	3 (19-1)

In Hand A, you play your non-working Queen early. Dealer, thinking you might have an Ace with your Queen-4, decides not to make the count 30, and decides to play his 3. You score 30-3. In Hand B, your first two cards played are 4-8. Dealer guesses you have a 3, and refuses to make the count 28, or to play his own 3.

Some would contend that it's better to save the non-working card for last. "She'll never guess your last card," they say. And they're right, she *won't* guess the card, but by the time you are down to only one card, it may be too late—as it was in Hand B—to gain any advantage from having kept her in the dark.

25

Save Your Pegging Cards

No, I don't mean save your four lowest cards. I mean, save the cards that allow you to use the strategies we've been discussing. Obviously you won't break up a good hand to save useful pegging cards, but when you have a choice between two equally useful (or useless) cards, keep the one that is most likely to help in the pegging game.

Holding A-4-6-6-7-Q, you'll probably decide to toss Dealer A-Q or 4-Q. If the cut is going to be an 8, you want to save the Ace. If the cut is going to be a 5, you want to save the 4. If you can't find a significant difference between saving the 4 or the Ace, you might save the 4 because it allows you to lead from three cards that total 16. If Dealer has all 10's and 5's, 4-6-6 will pay off in big pegging.

Imagine you are ten holes from victory, and Dealer needs only three or four holes. If Dealer gives you 2-3-4-6-9-K, you'd rather save 2-3-4-6 than 2-3-4-9, partly because you can lead from three cards that total 11. You have a chance at 15-2 and 31-2 if Dealer plays 10-cards. But if you are the Dealer, you might prefer to save 2-3-4-9. That 2-9 combination will pay off if Opponent plays face cards.

There will be plenty of opportunities to use most of the strategies we've discussed, but there'll be even more opportunities if you save cards that make using those strategies possible.

26

Offer Opponent 15 for 4

Suppose Opponent leads a 3, and you are holding 6-7-8-K (you tossed A-A, and the cut is a Queen). If Opponent needs only two holes to win the game, playing the 7 would allow him to peg out with a 5 or a 7. Playing the King lets him peg out with a King or a 2. Playing the 8 lets him peg out with an 8 or a 4. If you play your 6, he can peg out only with a 6. The 6 is clearly the best play.

What about earlier in the game? Earlier, if you're like most players, the one card you would not play is the 6, as this could give up 15-4. But let's look a bit more closely. If you play the 7, 8, or King, Opponent can peg two holes by pairing you, or two holes by scoring 15-2. In all, there are seven cards in the deck with which he might score two points. There are three cards in the deck (the remaining 6's) with which he might score four points if you play the 6. In other words, if you always play the 6 in this situation, Opponent will score twice as many points *when he scores*, but he will score less than half as often. In the long run you come out ahead playing the 6.

Your Opponent may even decide not to take the 15-4 on those occasions when he has a 6 of his own. Unless he thinks you're a complete novice, he may fear that the only reason you would offer this bonus is that you have two 6's, and are hoping to triple.

Of course you shouldn't always take this risk. If Opponent is four holes from victory, and you are two holes from victory, then you can't afford to risk losing immediately; you might be able to peg on Opponent's next card, and win the game.

Playing a 4 on Opponent's lead of a 7, or a 3 on his lead of a 9, are not recommended—if you can instead put the count above 15. When you can otherwise limit Opponent to one pegging card, don't risk giving up four holes. But playing a 6 on Opponent's lead of a 3, or a 7 on his Ace, are sound moves. If your position is such that you are happy to give up two holes, but can't stand to give up four, ignore this strategy. But if your goal is to hold Opponent's pegging to zero holes, your chances are better taking the risk.

27

Reevaluate Your Position
Often on 4th Street

On 4th Street, it's a good idea to plan ahead, but it's also a good idea to be ready to scrap your plans at a moment's notice. Suppose you're holding 2-3-5-6, with an 8 cut, both players are fourteen holes from home, and Opponent leads a 10. If Opponent has fourteen points, obviously you've lost, so your primary worry is that he has twelve points and needs to peg two. He could have 10-10-10-5 or 10-10-5-5, or even some hand with middle cards, like 6-7-8-10.

You try your 2, as you can't think of a twelve-point hand with 2-8-10. He pairs your 2. Now he's twelve holes from home, so your new worry is that he has a ten-point hand. He could have 2-5-5-10. If so, you can't play your 5 now.

Each time a card comes down, rethink your situation. If the board position or the view you've taken of Opponent's hand has changed, you may need to change your strategy. And this becomes more vital the closer you get to home.

Imagine you need seven holes and Dealer needs two. You pick up A-2-3-4-5-J, and decide to keep 2-3-4-J and to lead the 3. The cut is a 2, so you have plenty of points, if you can only keep Dealer from pegging two holes. Unfortunately, he pairs your 3 and wins. Unlucky, to be sure, but you might have had better luck if you'd played the percentages. When a 2 was cut, you should have changed your plan. Since you could see two 2's, Dealer was less likely to have a 2 than a 3. You should have led your 2.

Suppose you need two holes and Dealer needs three. You pick up 3-3-4-6-9-10, and save 3-4-6-9. Your plan is to lead the 6, secure in the knowledge that you can peg out if Dealer pairs you or scores 15-2. An excellent plan. You cut the deck, and Dealer turns over a Jack. Time out! That cut pushes Dealer two holes closer to home. You're safer leading the 3 now, as you were dealt two 3's, making that the card Dealer is least likely to peg on. Plan ahead, yes, but have the flexibility to change plans as each new piece of evidence is revealed.

28

Avoid Tossing Yourself Q-K

Touching cards have a better chance of becoming a run than "two-apart" cards. If you toss yourself 8-10, you need a 9 to form a run. If you toss yourself 9-10, you need either an 8 or a Jack—twice as likely. However, there is one special case worth mentioning. Suppose you hold A-A-4-10-Q-K. You might be inclined to toss yourself the touching Q-K, but in fact, you are better off tossing 10-Q. Either way you need a Jack as the cut (or from Opponent) to form a run in the crib. But suppose the cut *is* a Jack. J-Q-K can be extended only with a 10, while 10-J-Q can be extended with a 9 or a King. Your three-card run is more likely to become a four-card run if you've tossed 10-Q.

More to the point, if no Jack is cut or tossed to your crib, the King and Queen may prove worthless, but the 10 could be useful in forming a run or even a double run. It's not unheard of for Opponent to toss you 8-10 or 9-J. And if the cut is a 9, you'll be much happier if you've tossed 10-Q than if you've tossed Q-K.

What if it's not your crib? You may on occasion be tossing to Opponent's crib from among J-Q-K. Your hand may be 7-7-8-J-Q-K, or 2-2-3-J-Q-K, or even J-J-Q-Q-K-K. You may be inclined to give Dealer J-K, simply because they aren't touching cards. But not only could the Jack contribute to a 9-10-10-J double run; it could prove to be nobs. Toss him Q-K.

Let's look at the lower end of the card sequence. Is 2-4 a better toss than Ace-2? Maybe, but if those are the three cards from which you're choosing, your best toss to your own crib will usually be A-4, which, while less likely to form a run, is highly likely to contribute to one or more 15-2's.

And if it's Opponent's crib? Suppose you are holding A-2-4-8-8-8, and you must toss two cards to your Opponent. Not wanting to give up A-4, you must decide between A-2 and 2-4. And you are clearly better off tossing Dealer the touching cards, A-2. Either way he needs a 3 to complete a run, but if he gets the 3, the run will be extended more easily if it's 2-3-4 than if it's A-2-3. And, even without a 3, that 4 could help Dealer to a big crib. If Dealer tosses 5-6 into his crib, and you cut him a 5, his crib will contain two points if you've tossed A-2. It'll contain *twelve* points if you've tossed 2-4. Preventing a 4-5-6 double run in Dealer's crib is reason enough to toss A-2.

29

Lead the Deuce from 2-3-4

When you lead from 2-3, you are hoping Dealer will play a 10-card, giving you 15-2. And if Dealer is going to play a 10-card, it won't matter whether you've led the 2 or the 3. But Dealer won't want to play a 10 if he can safely avoid it. And the safest way to avoid it is by playing a middle card.

Because Dealer may be reluctant to play a 5 or a 6 on your lead of a 3, but won't mind playing either on your lead of a 2, the 3 is generally a better lead than the 2. It's more likely to force a 10-card. But the situation is a bit different when you have a 4 with your 2-3. With 2-3-4, you can lead the 2 and score 15-2 if Dealer plays a 10-card or a 9. You can lead the 3, and score 15-2 if Dealer plays a 10-card or an 8. Which is Dealer more likely to have and play? An 8 or a 9?

I contend that the 9 is a more popular card to save. In the first place, a 9 works with either low card run (A-2-3 or 2-3-4). The 9 works with the oft-held 4-5-6. And it can work with high cards (10-J-J) as well. The 8 is a bit less versatile. The 8 seldom ventures outside his immediate circle of friends, though he does bring a keg when his fellow middle cards have a party. The 9 is more likely to crash the little and big cards' parties, and chip in a six-pack.

Beyond the 9's popularity, players with both an 8 and a 9 tend to play the higher card when given a choice—especially if they have a 7, as they'll hope they can use the 7-8 to score a run or 15-2 at the tail end of the pegging.

The 9 is slightly more likely to be in Dealer's hand, and slightly more likely to be played on a low card lead. If you've been leading the 3 from 2-3-4, try switching to the 2. You may be pleasantly surprised at how often a 9 hits the other side of the table.

Bonus Tip

If Dealer is going to make a special effort to play a 9 when you lead a 2, you may as well lead the 2 from 2-4, even when you don't have a 3. He won't know you have no 3, that it's safe to play a 10-card. Likewise, if you lead the 3 from 3-4 even without a 2, Dealer will often play an 8, cleverly avoiding playing a 10-card, cleverly making the count 11 to annoy you, and cleverly playing right into your hands.

30

If a Certain Card Puts Opponent Out, Assume He Doesn't Have It

At the end of a cribbage game, you will occasionally encounter a situation in which your opponent needs a certain number of points to win the game, and has exposed three of his cards.

Opponent	**You**
Q	4 (14)
Q (24)	5 (29)
2 (31-2)	?

You are six holes from victory, your last two cards are a 3 and a 4, and the cut is a 3. It looks like Opponent's last card might be a 3, and early in the game you would play your 4 at this point. But late in the game, you should first note how close Opponent is to the game hole. Let's say that after pegging his 31-2, he is now eleven holes from home. It should be clear to you that if his last card is a 2, a 3, or a Queen, his hand is worth twelve points—enough points to win. *So you should assume he doesn't have a 2, 3, or Queen!* And once you've made this assumption, there's no reason not to play your own 3.

You may be thinking, *Assuming Opponent has no 3 does not necessarily make it so!* True enough. But if he does have a 3, and you let him pair your 3, it costs you nothing. He was going to win anyway, with his twelve-point hand. On the other hand, if you play your 4 and he pairs that, his hand (2-4-Q-Q) is worth nine points, and you've given him the other two points he needs.

More complicated examples of such problems will be seen later (Tip #35). For now, let's just say that at the end of the game, if there's a card you can't afford Opponent to have, your best strategy is to assume he doesn't have it.

31

For Extra Pegging,
Keep Touching Cards Until Last

We saw in Tip #22 how to trap Opponent's 5 into a three-card run by holding onto 3-4, 4-6, or 6-7. Well, you aren't going to have those cards all of the time, and for that matter, Opponent isn't going to have a 5 all of the time. You can still trap a card in Opponent's hand, however, by hanging onto touching cards.

In the hand below, you hang onto your 7-8, hoping to trap either a 6 or a 9:

Opponent	You
10	2 (12)
J (22)	2 (24)
5 (29-2)	8
9 (17)	7 (24-4)

Opponent didn't make a mistake. He'd have been better off playing his 9 earlier, but he had no way of knowing that was the case.

Opponent	You
J	5 (15-2)
10 (25)	6 (31-2)
?	

Opponent's last two cards are 3-9. If he plays the 3, and your last two cards are 7-8 or 8-10, you've trapped his 9. If he plays his 9 first, and your last two cards are 4-5, 2-4, or A-2, you've trapped his 3. What can he do? By saving touching cards, or two-apart cards, you are sure to occasionally pick up three extra holes.

The most common cards to trap, besides the 5, are the Jack—the 10-card Opponent is least likely to toss into your crib—and the Ace—the card Opponent is least likely to play early.

You don't have to be the Dealer to score with touching cards:

You	Dealer
K	9 (19)
5 (24)	2 (26)
Go	4 (30-1)
J	9 (19)
10 (29-4)	

Had you played the Jack or the 10 first, instead of the King, you'd have lost out on three points.

Sometimes you don't even need a contribution from Opponent to score a run with touching cards, as in the next two examples:

Opponent	You	Opponent	You
4	8 (12)	6	K (16)
Q (22)	Go	6 (22)	3 (25)
4 (26)		Go	2 (27)
A (27-1)	J		A (28-4)
	Q (20)		
	K (30-4)		

Note that you can form runs with high touching cards, or with low touching cards. Some players, when they need to peg several holes, make a point of saving their lowest cards. This may work, depending on what Opponent has. But you're better off hanging onto touching cards, whether they're low cards or not.

32

Save Pairs and 15-2's to Peg Extra Holes

This tip could have been tacked onto the previous tip, so think of it as Tip #31B if you wish. In Tip #31, you tried to hold onto touching cards, hoping for extra points at the end of play. But you won't always have touching cards, and even when you do, you'll sometimes have to play one of them early. You can, however, still score if you've managed to hold onto a pair or a 15-2.

A		**B**	
Opponent	**You**	**Opponent**	**You**
3	8 (11)	6	Q (16)
4 (15-2)	7 (22)	6 (22)	A (23)
4 (26)	Go	7 (30-1)	2
2 (28-1)	9	2 (4-2)	2 (6-7)
	9 (18-3)		

In Hand A, holding your pair pays off, as Opponent is forced to play all of his cards, allowing you to play your 9's consecutively. Had you played your 9's first, your 15-2 (7-8) would have scored for you at the end. You're better off holding onto the pair than the 15-2, because the count must be 0 to score with your 15-2. Pairs also tend to pay off a bit more often than touching cards, but keep in mind that touching cards pay off with three or more holes, not just two.

Sometimes you'll save a pair, and Opponent won't be forced to play all of his cards. You can still get lucky—his last card may match your pair, as in Hand B.

It's easy to peg if Opponent continuously plays cards that allow you to score 15-2's, runs, and pairs. But Opponent can't be relied upon to assist you. Sometimes you have to do it on your own, and the best way is to hang onto your pairs, 15-2's, and touching cards.

33

To Limit Opponent's Pegging, Keep a Diversity of Cards

It's the last hand of the game. You need twelve points to win; your Opponent needs seventeen. Tension is high. Opponent leads out with a 3. You look down at your cards and realize, too late, that it was probably a mistake to save 2-2-4-4. Opponent (with A-3-3-5) has no trouble pegging eleven holes, and the cut, a 3, gives him eight points, more than enough to win.

Perhaps your original hand was 2-2-4-4-6-8. Any other time in the game, tossing the 6-8 in your crib would make sense. You don't want to lose a potential 18-point hand. Well, you got your cut for the 18-point hand. Happy?

You'd have been better off holding 2-2-6-8. On the lead of a 3 you can play the 8. On the lead of a 7, you can play a 2. It's always nice to have as many choices as possible when trying to limit Opponent's pegging.

Of course, you can't always afford to keep a diversity of cards; you do need some points most of the time. But you can still try to play your cards in an order that preserves as wide a spread as possible. If you have a pair, play from it early so you have more choices later. If you have a run, play the middle card early, maintaining the "wide" spread of the outer cards.

In the following hand, Opponent is five holes from victory. You hope he has a poor hand, but if he does, you still have to do what you can to keep him from pegging. Your hand is 2-7-8-9, and the cut is an Ace.

Opponent	You
K	8 (18)
K (28)	2 (30-1)
10	

Having unloaded the middle card of your run, you now have a safe play on Opponent's 10: your 7. Had you played the 7 earlier, instead of the 8, you'd now be offering him a three-card run, and if his hand is K-K-10-9, he would peg enough to win. Had you played the 9 earlier, instead of the 8, you'd be safe from Opponent's 10, but what if he had played a 6 instead of the 10? You'd be down to 7-8, and in danger of giving up three or four pegging holes to K-K-6-7.

Opponent will occasionally be kind enough to save fewer points than he needs. Don't repay his kindness by helping him peg the points he lacks.

34

Play a 5 on Opponent's Lead of . . . an 8?

Here's a tip that won't pay off in points very often, but it's harmless to try it, and when it does pay off, it's usually because Opponent has a good hand. Holding a 5, you naturally hope to see Opponent lead out with a face card. Often he obliges. When he doesn't, you usually refrain from playing the 5, hoping it will come in handy later. But interesting things can happen when you play a 5 on Opponent's 8.

Think about what always happens to you when you lead an 8.

You	Dealer
8	7 (15-2)
9 (24-3)	6 (30-5)

And the pain continues through the next two cards. If you have middle cards (6's, 7's, 8's, and 9's), and Dealer has them as well, Dealer usually makes out like a bandit. Many expert players try to avoid leading middle cards if possible.

Of course, hands with lots of middle cards score very well, so when your opponent has them, he keeps them. Thus, when Opponent leads an 8, it's reasonable to guess that he might have something like 7-8-8-9 or 6-7-8-8, and had no choice but to lead a middle card. You hope he doesn't have one of those hands, but my opponents seem to get those hands a lot, so I assume yours do too. What happens if you play a 5 on Opponent's 8?

Opponent	You
8	5 (13)
?	

A 7 doesn't look too attractive to him, as it would allow you to score a four-card run with a 6, and to follow that with a 4 or a 5, either of which will get you at least five more holes.

A 9 would make the count 22, giving up 31-4 to a 9 in your hand.

An 8 would make the count 21—not especially attractive when the only card he's seen you play so far is a 5.

An Ace (from A-6-6-8, perhaps) would make the count 14, giving up 15-4 to an Ace in your hand.

A 6 looks better. True, you can still score a four-card run and then a five card run if you have a 7 and a 4 (3-4-5-7 might be your hand, or 4-5-6-7), but he'll assume that if you had a 7, you'd have used it to score 15-2. And you probably would have, but would that have been your best play?

A		B	
Opponent	**You**	**Opponent**	**You**
8	7 (15-2)	8	5! (13)
6 (21-3)	5 (26-4)	6 (19)	7 (26-4)
Go	4 (30-6)	Go	4 (30-6)

In hand B, Opponent, holding 6-7-8-8, decides that the 6 is the safest play on your 5, because you "obviously" don't have a 7. Surprise! You outpeg him by ten holes, whereas you outpeg him by nine when you score the 15-2.

Now, granted, the 8 he leads will sometimes be Opponent's only middle card—that won't bother you a bit. And granted, Opponent will usually have at least one safe play when you put a 5 on his 8, even if he has all middle cards. But he won't know *which play is safe*. If he makes the count 21 with an 8, and your hand is A-4-5-10, he'll wish he'd played anything but his 8. If he makes the count 22 with a 9, and your hand is A-A-5-9, he'll wish he'd played anything but his 9. And if he makes the count 19 or 20, and your hand is 4-5-6-7, he'll truly be kicking himself.

Your 5, if it does nothing else, will temporarily annoy him. And isn't that what cribbage is all about?

35

Having Seen Three of Opponent's Cards, Determine His Hand Value If He Can Peg With His Fourth

This tip will often prove useful on 4th Street, when the game is on the line. It's a slightly more complicated version of Tip #30. Suppose you need ten holes to win, and Opponent needs six. You deal yourself 2-3-4-6-10-J, and toss the 10-J into your crib. The cut is a 2, giving you twelve points. Now your only concern is that Opponent might go out before you get to count your hand. The play proceeds as follows:

Opponent	You (2-3-4-6)
Q	6 (16)
J (26)	4 (30-1)
3	?

Opponent's Jack is the same suit as the cut, so he has five points showing. Should you pair the 3, or play your 2?

This is not a guess, there's a right answer, though it takes a few moments to figure out. First of all, we can agree that it doesn't matter which card you play, if Opponent can't peg on either of your cards. So let's see what happens if Opponent can peg on one of your cards.

If you play the 2, Opponent can peg two holes with any 10-card or with a 2 of his own. He can also peg three holes with a 4 (we know he doesn't have an ace, so we don't worry about his pegging with an ace). But look! If Opponent has any 10-card or a 2 or a 4, his hand is worth at least eight points. In other words, if he can peg on your 2, he doesn't need to—he already has the game won with the points in his hand. Clearly it can't affect the outcome of the game to play your 2.

If you play your 3, Opponent can peg six holes with a 3 of his own, or he can score 15-2 with a 9. If his last card is a 3, he has eleven points, and has this game won. But if his last card is a 9, he has only five points, and is sitting there desperately willing you to play a 3 or a 9. Don't oblige him!

The key point is that it doesn't matter whether you play your 2 or your 3 *unless Opponent's last card is a 9*, so you may as well assume that he has a 9.

Let's look at the same situation:

Cut: 2

Opponent	You
Q	6 (16)
J (26)	4 (30-1)
3	?

Again you have enough points to go out, but last time, Opponent was six holes from home. This time, he needs eleven. Does this affect your decision?

It should. If Opponent can peg on your 3, he either has a 9, in which case his hand is worth five points, and he will lose, or he has a 3, in which case his hand is worth eleven points, and he will win. Either way, you can't affect the outcome.

But if Opponent can peg on your 2, his last card could be any 10-card. A 10-card would give him nine or ten points, and if you also let him score 15-2, you've given the game away. Play the 3!

What if Opponent had needed seventeen holes to win? Does your decision matter now? Yes. If Opponent's last card is a 3, he has eleven points. And if you let him triple your 3, you've given him the other six points he needs. You should play the 2.

Obviously it's Opponent's position on the board that determines which of your cards is most dangerous. Here's another sample hand: you hold 3-9-10-10, and are eight holes from victory. You tossed a pair of Kings into your crib, and the cut is a 6.

The play has proceeded:

Cut: 6

Opponent	You
6	10 (16)
3 (19)	10 (29-1)
6	?

Note your refusal to score 15-2, fearing that if Opponent had a 6, he might also have a 9. Your remaining cards are 3-9.

1. What do you play if Opponent needs 20 holes?

2. What do you play if Opponent needs 22 holes?

3. What do you play if Opponent needs 26 holes?

Solutions

1. Play the 3. If he can peg on that, he already has at least 20 points. But if you play your 9, and he pairs it, he has eighteen points, and you've given him the other two he needs.

2. Play the 9. If you play the 3, and Opponent pairs you, his hand is worth twenty points, and you've given him the game.

3. Play the 9. If you play the 3, and Opponent has a 6, he scores 15-2, and his hand is worth twenty-four points.

Note that to solve these problems at the table, you need to know how to mentally calculate the value of cribbage hands. You have to know what Opponent's hand is worth if he has 3-6-6-6 (24), 3-3-6-6 (20), or 3-6-6-9 (18). If that's a weakness for you, then practice, practice, practice.

36

Lead that 5! (I)

Not necessarily on opening lead—though it can be argued that there are situations in which an opening lead of a 5 is reasonable—but when the count has *returned* to 0.

Let's look at a couple of situations in which both you and the dealer have played some cards, the count is back to 0, and you have a 5. One reason to play the 5 is because Dealer's exposed cards lead you to believe that playing your 5 is the safest play. This could be the case if Dealer is attempting to trap your 5, as in the following hand:

You	Dealer
Q	9 (19)
J (29)	2 (31-2)
?	

Your last two cards are 5-K. If you suspect Dealer's last two cards are 3-4, 4-6, or 6-7—any of which is reasonable with his 2-9—play your 5 now, and retain your King. If Dealer's hand turns out to be 2-9-10-J, you'll feel silly, but at least you have a better hand than he does.

Even if your 5 is not being trapped, you may feel that Opponent is less likely to peg on it than on your other card.

You	Dealer
K	8 (18)
5 (23)	6 (29)
Go	A (30-1)
?	

Your last two cards are 5-6. Though it's certainly possible Dealer kept a 10-card with his A-6-8, it appears more likely that he has a 6 or a 9 than a 10-card. So you should lead the 5. It never feels comfortable making the count 5 (or 21), but sometimes it's the right play.

In the endgame, the 5 may prove to be the safest play. Suppose your last two cards are 3-5. Dealer also has two remaining cards, and the count is 0. You have enough points to go out, but no chance of pegging out. If you lead the 5, Dealer could peg as many as seven holes (if his cards are 3-3). If you lead the 3, Dealer could peg *eight* holes (if his cards are 3-4). Obviously, if Dealer is eight holes from home, leading the 5 is the only play that makes sense.

When the count gets back to 0, don't automatically reach for the other card when your last two cards include a 5. The 5 will be a reasonable play more often than you might think.

37

Strive to Reach Advantageous Positions

It's nice to have the lead in a cribbage game, but at the end of the game, having first count or the deal can be more important than having the lead. If one player is five holes from victory, and the other is six, which player do you want to be? You want to be the one with first count. If one player is fifteen holes from victory, and the other is seventeen, you'd prefer to be the one dealing.

Your position is considered favorable if you expect to win from that position with both players getting average cards. As Dealer, your average hand may consist of three holes pegged, ten points in your hand, and five points in the crib, for a total of eighteen points. Another Dealer might average twenty, or sixteen. Whether you average more or fewer depends in large part on your skill level and your opponents' skill levels.

Once you have an idea how far you tend to move on one hand, you'll know what constitutes a good position. If you average ten holes as nondealer, you'd like to be within ten holes of home when you have first count. How do you arrange this?

Let's say you are 26 holes from home, and Opponent is 18 holes from home. You deal yourself 2-6-7-8-10-K, and toss 10-K in your crib. The cut is a 3. With seven points, and no reason to be optimistic about your crib, you should peg at every opportunity. If you peg only one hole, and find three points in your crib, you'll be fifteen holes out starting the next hand. Not good. So, if Opponent leads a 2 or a 6, pair it. Those two holes may be crucial next hand.

If the cut was a 7, rather than a 3, giving you sixteen points, you are already within the 10-hole range of home. Even if you peg only one hole and find nothing in your crib, you'll still need only average cards to win. So if Opponent leads a 2 or a 6, lay off. Why risk the possibility he'll triple, and then go out with a big hand?

Here's another example. You deal, twenty holes from home. Opponent is eighteen holes from home. The cut is a 7, and you have tossed 2-3 into your crib.

Opponent	You
J	Q! (20)
10 (30-3)	A (31-2)
J	4 (14)
9 (23-1)	K (10-1)

Knowing that you had only four points, and that the cut didn't help your toss, you felt you would come up short of a favorable position. Thus you baited Opponent into taking a three-card run, just so you could score 31-2. You scored one point more than you otherwise would have. If you find five points in your crib, you'll start the next hand ten holes from home instead of eleven. Will that matter? Probably not, but it could. It could be the difference between winning and losing. Note that if the cut had been an Ace or a 4, giving you ten points and helping your crib, you'd never have risked giving up three points to Opponent.

To summarize, decide how far from home you need to be in order to win with average cards. Some players go so far as to assess their position before every hand, even on 1st Street! If you've already reached a winning position, play defensively. If you're short of your winning position, peg like a maniac, even if it means letting Opponent peg extra holes. Because if you go into the last hand needing above-average cards, you'll be disappointed more often than not.

38

Assume Dealer Won't Peg on Your Lead

We saw earlier (Tip #12) that it's a good idea to expect Dealer to peg on your lead. From 3-4-5-7, you lead the 4, because you expect Dealer to pair you, and you know your 7 will let you regain the two points.

So, when is it right to expect Dealer *not* to peg on your lead? When Dealer needs only two holes to win the game! In that situation, you can't regain the points Dealer scores, because the game is over.

I'm not suggesting, when I say, "Assume Dealer won't peg on your lead," that the power of positive thinking will prevent Dealer from pegging. I'm saying that when faced with playing from two or more cards that Dealer is equally likely to peg on, there's a better way of choosing your lead than mere intuition.

Let's say that both you and the Dealer need two holes to win. From 2-4-7-9-Q-K you save 2-4-7-9, and the cut is a 10. Naturally you narrow your opening lead choice down to the 2 and the 4. How do you decide which to lead? Let's look at the possible scenarios.

1. Dealer has both a 2 *and* a 4.

2. Dealer has neither a 2 *nor* a 4.

3. Dealer has one but not the other.

In scenario 1, Dealer will peg on your opening lead and win the game. In scenario 2, Dealer will not peg on your lead, and will play a card that you might be able to peg on. In scenario 3, Dealer will peg on your lead half the time.

The scenarios we are concerned with are those in which Dealer doesn't peg on your opening lead. How can you maximize the chances that Dealer will play a card that you can peg on? By assuming from the start that he won't peg on whichever card you play, and determining which cards he might play that will allow you to peg on him.

From 2-4-7-9, if you lead the 4 you'll peg if Dealer plays a 2, 7, or 9. You'll pair him. If you lead the 2, you'll not only pair a 4, 7, or 9, you'll also score 15-2 if Dealer plays a 6. An extra chance. So the 2 is a better lead. Earlier in the game you might have led the 4, knowing you could score 15-2 if Dealer paired you.

Suppose both you and Dealer need two holes to win, and you must lead from A-2-3-4. Which is best? Dealer can probably pair one or two of those cards, but you have no way of knowing which, so you assume he won't pair you. No matter which card you lead, you will score 15-2 if Dealer plays a 10-card. If you lead the 2, you'll also score 15-2 if Dealer plays a 9. If you lead the 3, you'll score 15-2 if Dealer plays an 8. But if you lead the 4, you'll score 15-2 if Dealer plays an 8 *or* a 9. So the 4 is your best lead.

If you lead the 4 and Dealer's hand is 4-J-Q-K, you'll realize, after he pairs your 4, that any other lead would have won the game for you. At such times, console yourself with the knowledge that if you don't lose occasionally, no one will want to play with you.

39

If Opponent Needs Two, Offer Him Three

The strategy we discussed in Tip #38 is not exclusive to the opening leader. Dealer may have a chance to use it as well. Again, let's assume both you and Opponent need two points to win. If you can't pair the opening lead, you play the safest card possible. If you can restrict Opponent to one pegging card you do so (playing a 7 on an Ace, playing a 10 on a 6, etc.). Otherwise, you try to restrict him to two possible pegging cards. This usually means restricting him to pairing or scoring 15-2, and not letting him have the extra chance of scoring a run.

However, if the lead was an Ace, 2, or 3, you may be able to restrict Opponent from scoring 15-2 by playing a low card of your own. If the opening lead is an Ace, and you hold 2-3-4-6, consider playing the 2 or the 3. Why offer three points instead of two? Why not? He only needs two points anyway. The key is, if he can't peg on your card, he can't put the count above 15. If you play the 2 on his Ace, what will he do? You'll peg out if he plays an Ace, 4, 6, 8, or 9. If you play the 3 on his Ace you'll peg out if he plays an Ace, 4, 5, 6, 7, or 9.

Yes, if you play the 6 on his Ace, there are many cards he can play to let you peg out, but he will put the count above 15 if he can, restricting you to one possible pegging card. When keeping the count below 5 is no more danger-ous than putting it above, play low.

40

Holding 3 Cards to Opponent's 1, THINK!

During the play of the hand, you'll occasionally find yourself holding three cards while your Opponent holds only one. If you have a pair, you'll be tempted to lead from that pair, hoping Opponent's last card will match the pair, giving you six holes for tripling, plus two Go's. Here's an example:

Opponent	You
7	K (17)
6 (23)	Go
8 (31-2)	?

Your last three cards are J-J-Q. Your first thought in this situation may be something like this:

I haven't been able to triple this guy all night, because he never pairs me, but now he has only one card, and if that card is a Jack, he'll be forced to pair me, and I'll get my triple. Besides, even if his last card is a Queen, it's still better to play a Jack, so I can pair his Queen. Playing a Jack is a win-win situation!

So you play a Jack. If you had thought a bit longer, you'd have realized that there is one card Opponent might be holding which would make leading the Queen advantageous. What is that card?

That's right, an Ace. If Opponent has an Ace, you can score 31-4 by playing the Queen first, and saving the Jacks. And, while Opponent's desire to throw trash into your crib may have forced him to save any card with that 6-7-8, an Ace certainly seems more likely than a Jack or a Queen, simply because an Ace improves the hand, and could improve it even more with a favorable cut.

Here's another example. As Dealer, you hold 7-8-9-9.

Opponent	You
Q	7 (17)
Q (27)	Go
3 (30-1)	?

Your first thought is to play a 9, because if Opponent is forced to pair, you'll triple. But my money is on Opponent having a 2 or a 5 with his 3-Q-Q, in which case the 6 is the better play, as you'll get to pair your own 9.

In this final example, misreading the situation could cost *more* than two holes:

Opponent	You
K	9 (19)
Q (29)	Go
2 (31-2)	?

Your remaining cards are 3-3-6. It looks like Opponent might have a 3, so it's tempting to play a 3. But look closely. If Opponent does have a 3, and you start with your 3, you'll peg six holes with your other 3, and score 15-3 with your 6. Opponent gets two holes for pairing your 3. If you start with your 6, however, Opponent gets nothing, while you score two points for pairing his 3, and 15-9 with your second 3. Plus, when Opponent *doesn't* have a 3, you still gain two points by retaining the pair and pairing your own 3.

When holding 3 cards (including a pair) to Opponent's one, consider whether it's likely that all four remaining cards can be played without going over 31. If they can, it's usually best to hang onto your pair in hopes of playing them consecutively.

41

Lead that 5! (II)

Leading a 5 as your opening seems silly, and in most cases it is. It's easy enough to construct hands on which this lead works out, but easier still to construct hands on which it doesn't.

One situation in which it's reasonably safe to lead a 5 is when you also hold three different 10-cards. There's a strong likelihood Dealer will score 15-2, but there's also a strong likelihood you can pair his 10-card. What you're hoping will happen is this:

You	Dealer
5	J (15-2)
J (25-2)	4 (29)
Go	A (30-1)
Q	J (20)
K (30-4)	

What you're hoping *won't* happen is this:

You	Dealer
5	10 (15-2)
K (25)	3 (28)
Go	2 (30)
	A (31-5)
Q	
J (20-1)	

The problem with leading a 5 from 5-10-J-Q is that your hand becomes an open book. Oh, sure, for a brief moment Dealer may think you're holding 5-5-5-5, but then he'll realize it's more likely you have 5-10-J-Q, and he may be able to use this knowledge to his advantage. Holding 6-9-10-J, knowing you'll likely pair his 10-card if he plays one, he may play his 6, making the count 11.

Now you have to guess which 10-card to play to keep him from scoring 31-4.

Or, perhaps Dealer holds 5-6-7-9. He sees you lead a 5. He's confident you have three 10-cards, and that he can pair your 5 safely, outpegging you by three holes. However, knowing your entire hand, he quickly deduces that he can play his 9 on your 5 and outpeg you by six holes.

When is leading a 5 worth the risk? Suppose you hold 5-10-J-Q, and need thirteen holes to win. Dealer also needs thirteen. The cut, unfortunately, is a 3, and not the right 3. You need to peg four holes. Lead the 5. Dealer may have nothing but face cards. Needing thirteen holes, what would he save if he was dealt A-2-J-Q-Q-K? Would he risk saving only two or three points?

You	Dealer
5	K (15-2)
K (25-3)	Q (10)
Q (20-2)	Q (30-7)
J	J (20-3)

True, you lost the pegging duel by seven holes, but leading the 5 got you the holes you needed to go out with your nine-point hand. Fortunately, Dealer didn't quite manage to peg out. Had you led a face card, Dealer might have paired it, in which case you would not have pegged more than three holes.

42

Avoid Run Traps

When Opponent plays the last card, you want him to get one point. If the count happens to be 31, you'll let him take two. But you don't want him getting three extra points for forming a run with that last card. Can you do anything to prevent it? We've discussed dumping the 5 to keep it from being trapped into a run. But since Opponent won't always have the means to trap a 5, he may go after another card in your hand by saving his touching cards. If avoiding a run trap is a priority, the following general ideas may be helpful.

The play of the hand consists of one or more "cycles," each of which ends at or below a count of 31. If the last cycle consists of three cards, Dealer holding two while you hold one, there's no foolproof means of ensuring that your card isn't trapped into a run. You can reduce the chances of a run trap, however, in two ways:

1. Hang on to an Ace or a King as your last card, or, if that's not an option, to a 2 or a Queen. A King can be trapped into a run only by J-Q. A Jack can be trapped by 9-10, 10-Q, or Q-K. If you can play your Jack early and retain your King, you're in less danger.

2. If you've noticed that your Opponent doesn't have a certain card, you can reduce his chances of trapping you. For instance, if your opening lead was a 6, and Opponent didn't score 15-2, he probably has no 9. If you save an 8 as your last card, he can trap you with 6-7, but probably not with 7-9 or 9-10.

Of course, there's no certainty that the last cycle to 31 will consist of three cards. Often the count will revert to 0 after you and Dealer have each played two cards. In such cases, you can't be trapped into a run if your two cards are both 9's or higher. If you can't save two high cards, one may be enough, depending on your other card. If your high card is a King or Queen, you need a 2 or higher with it. Lead the 2, and Opponent can't use your high card to form a run. If your high card is a Jack, you'll need to lead a 3 or higher to prevent Opponent from scoring a run with 9-10. Always remember to lead the lower card; if you lead the J from 3-J, Opponent can trap your 3. Keep those high cards, and you may not get trapped so often.

43

Watch the Suits of Opponent's Cards

The suits of the cards don't score points in the pegging phase of the game, but that doesn't mean you should ignore them. If you suspect your opponent has a flush, you have valuable information about his hand.

Say your opponent leads a King, and the play proceeds:

Opponent	You
K	7 (17)
Q (27)	2 (29-1)
J	?

You must play either the 6 of clubs or the 8 of hearts. If all three of Opponent's cards are hearts, you would play the 8. You suspect that he has a flush, and if he does, he can't possibly pair your 8. If all of his cards are clubs, you would play the 6, again fearing that he has a flush. Why would Opponent save a 6 or an 8 with his J-Q-K? One possible reason is that it gives him a flush!

Here are two additional examples:

A		**B**	
Opponent	**You**	**You**	**Dealer**
6	J (16)	9	K (19)
4 (20)	Q (30-1)	3 (22)	5 (27)
2	?	Go	4 (31-2)
		?	

In hand A, your last two cards are the 10 of clubs and the King of hearts. Obviously the card you play won't matter if Opponent has anything besides a 10 or a King. Opponent seems equally likely (or unlikely) to have either card, as neither would help his hand. Which do you play? This is an easy decision if Opponent's 2, 4, and 6 are all hearts. If Opponent does have a flush, he can't possibly have a King, so you play your King. And of course if

Opponent's 2, 4 and 6 are all clubs, you play the 10.

In hand B, Opponent dealt, but you've still come down to the same situation. You hold the 7 of hearts and the 8 of spades. If Dealer's cards are all hearts, play the 7. If his cards are all spades, play the 8. If he has a flush, he can't pair you, and if he scores 15-2, you get to pair him.

BONUS TIP

We've just seen how noticing that Opponent's first three cards are the same suit can aid in deciding which card to play. Well, when you hold *three* cards of the same suit, play them first, and your opponent may become so concerned with your "flush" that he makes the wrong play. Here's an example:

You hold the 6-10-J of diamonds, and the 10 of spades. You lead off with a 10, *making sure that it's the 10 of diamonds*. The play proceeds:

You	Dealer
10	5 (15-2)
J (25)	6 (31-2)
6	?

Dealer's last two cards are the King of hearts and the 10 of clubs. Normally in this situation he would play the King, because it seems more likely that you have a 10 than a King. After all, a 10 gives you two points, while a King is worthless to your hand. But he notices that all of your cards are diamonds. He knows you can't pair his 10 if you have a flush, because you've already played the 10 of diamonds. But you *could* pair his King if you have a flush—with the King of diamonds. The King of *diamonds* would give your hand a value of four points. He squirms in his seat, mops his brow, and plays . . . the 10! Had you led the 10 of *spades* earlier, Dealer would have had no reason to believe you might have a King, and probably would have played his own King.

44

Toss Similar Cards
When You Must Blank Dealer's Crib

The cards in a deck may be divided into four categories for cribbage purposes: low cards, middle cards, high cards, and 5's. If Dealer can't toss a 5 into his crib, he often tries to toss two cards from the same category. He's hoping you, too, will toss at least one card from that category. If he tosses 7-8, he's hoping you'll toss 6-10 or 9-K, and that the cut will give him ten or twelve points. Non-dealer, of course, tries to toss cards from different categories. True, this means one of his cards is more likely to fit with Dealer's toss, but chances are they won't *both* fit, and Dealer won't have a huge crib.

However, toward the end of a game, you may reach a position in which you can't stand for Dealer to have *any* points in his crib. And in such situations, you are better off tossing two cards from the *same* category.

Let's say Dealer needs sixteen holes to win, and you need twenty-five. Your chances are bleak enough, and if you let Dealer have a six-point crib, you have almost no chance. Holding 2-2-7-9-J-Q, you might consider 7-Q as a reasonable toss. Early in the game, your thinking would be, *Dealer might be tossing 5-Q, or he might be tossing 7-8. If I toss 7-9 or J-Q, I could get burned for sixteen or more. By tossing 7-Q, I prevent the huge crib.*

True enough, but if Dealer is tossing 5-Q or 7-8, and you toss 7-Q, he'll score at least six points. And at this stage of the game, you aren't trying to prevent a sixteen crib; you're trying to prevent a six crib. Your best bet is to toss 7-9 and hope Dealer is tossing Q-K, or to toss J-Q and hope Dealer is tossing 6-8. Yes, some of the time you'll guess wrong and give Dealer a dozen, but if he gets a dozen, chances are he'd have had half that much if you'd tossed from two different categories. And since he's likely to move at least six holes with his hand and pegging, he'd have been in excellent shape to win with first count next hand.

Remember, you're making this play in a game you expect to lose anyway. Your goal is to give yourself a chance. If you can give Opponent a blank crib, you might get to count your own crib next hand. Hope it's loaded!

45

Keep the Safest Card (I)

Often Opponent will say, "Go," and you'll be holding two cards, either (but not both) of which you can play without reaching 31. Since either card will get you one point, your decision regarding which card to play should depend on which card you want to retain in your hand. Suppose you are holding 2-4-6-J, and the cut is a 5. The play proceeds, as follows:

You	Dealer
4	J (14)
J (24-2)	Go
?	

Should you play the 2 or the 6? Your reasoning might be, *Let's see, both of Dealer's cards are 8's or higher. That means no matter which card I retain, he won't be able to pair it or form a run with it, or score a 15-2 with it. I'm safe. On the other hand, he could lead a 9 now, and I would score 15-2 if I've played the 2 and retained the 6.*

Well-reasoned if it's early in the game, but let's imagine that you need six points to win, and Dealer needs only two holes. Is there any danger in playing the 2? Yes. If you retain the 6, you are guaranteed to lose! Dealer will peg out. Remember, his cards are all 8's or higher. If you retain the 6, he'll score 30-3 if he has three 8's, he'll score 31-2 if he has 8-8-9, and he'll score two Go's if he has anything else.

You	Dealer
4	J (14)
J (24-2)	Go
2 (26-1)	8
6 (14)	9 (23-1)
	K (10-1)

Your only hope of winning is to play the 6, retain the 2, and hope that Opponent's last three cards are 8-9-10, or 8-Q-K, or 8-10-J, etc., holding him to only one Go.

Now let's assume Dealer needs three holes instead of two. Does this change your strategy? Yes! Now you need to play the 2 and retain the 6! You no longer care if Dealer gets two Go's or 31-2; now you need to prevent him from winning if he has a pair of 9's, 10's, Jack's, Queens, or Kings. You need to drive the count high enough so that he can't play the cards of his pair consecutively. You wouldn't want to see this happen:

You	Dealer
4	J (14)
J (24-2)	Go
6 (30-1)	9
2 (11)	10 (21)
	10 (31-4)

You can still lose if Dealer has 8-8-8 or 8-8-9, but that would be true whether you retained the 2 *or* the 6.

Whether it's right to keep the count low, hoping to prevent Dealer from getting two Go's, or to drive it higher, *forcing* two Go's, can depend on a one-hole difference in Dealer's position. Stay alert!

46

Keep the Safest Card (II)

Sometimes it's the dealer who must choose between two cards after Opponent has said, "Go."

Opponent	You
6	9 (15-2)
2 (17)	9 (26)
Go	?

Your last two cards are a 3 and a 4. The cut is an 8. Which card do you play?

Let's think this through. Opponent's cards are both higher than a 5. Thus, no matter which card you retain, he will not be able to pair it or form a run. And since he has only two cards, the count won't get high enough to reach 31 on the next cycle. So is there any danger here? Hey, this is cribbage! There's *always* danger.

If you play the 4 and retain the 3, Opponent could score 15-3 if his last two cards are 6-6:

Opponent	You
6	9 (15-2)
2 (17)	9 (26)
Go	4 (30-1)
6	3 (9)
6 (15-3)	

If you play the 3 and retain the 4, however, there are no two cards—both higher than a 5—that could combine with your 4 to make the count 15. In other words, if you play the 3, Dealer later gets a Go; if you play the 4, he later gets a Go, and he *could* get a 15-2 as well. The choice is obvious.

This type of situation can become complicated. In the next hand, the end of the game is near, and the cut is a 3.

You have enough points to go out, thanks to the cut.

Opponent	You
3	9 (12)
6 (18)	9 (27)
Go	?

Your remaining cards are 2-3. If you retain the 2, Opponent will score 15-2 with 6-7 or 5-8. If you retain the 3, he'll score 15-2 with 6-6 or 5-7. So how do you decide? Fortunately, you know exactly how many points he has if he has any of those combinations. If he has 6-7, his hand is worth eight points. If he has 5-8 it's worth two points. 6-6 would give him twenty points, and 5-7 would give him nine points.

How does this help? If Opponent is twenty-two holes from victory, unload the 3 and retain the 2. You can't risk his scoring 15-3 if he has the twenty-point hand (3-6-6-6). If Opponent needs four points to win, unload the 2 and retain the 3. You can't risk his scoring 15-3 if he has the two-point hand (3-5-6-8). And so on.

BONUS TIP

For additional examples, visit www.Cribbageforum.com, and click on pegging/endgames, then on "defending against a two-on-one."

While you're at the site, you can also click on "Ask the Experts," where I and several other so-called experts consistently disagree on the best way one might handle specific cribbage situations.

47

Guard Against the Worst That Can Happen

Sometimes you'll be lucky enough to have first count with enough points to go out, and Dealer needs more than a couple points. Don't become complacent. Even when the game is seemingly won, figure out whether Opponent has a slight chance of victory. If he does, do what you can to prevent it.

You have first count, needing eight holes to win. Dealer needs ten holes. You save 2-3-4-K, and the cut is a 4, so you have enough points to go out. And you feel great. The play proceeds:

You	Dealer
2	7 (9)
K (19)	Q (29-1)
?	

Dealer is more likely to peg on your 3 than your 4, as you can see two 4's. But put that thought out of your mind—it's irrelevant in this situation. You should concern yourself only with what might happen to allow Dealer to peg nine more holes.

What could happen next if you play the 4? The worst possible sequence is in Hand A:

A			**B**	
You	**Dealer**		**You**	**Dealer**
4	3 (7)		3	4 (7)
3 (10-2)	3 (13-7)		4 (11-2)	4 (15-9)

Dealer pegs seven more holes—eight in all. Unpleasant for you, but you still win the game.

What could happen if you play the 3? In Hand B, Dealer pegs ten holes in all, and you lose a game you should have won. If one play guarantees victory, and the other can cost you the game, the decision is easy.

Earlier, at the end of Tip #21, we saw a near-miraculous finish—Dealer pegging nine holes to pull out a seemingly lost game:

Opponent	Dealer
3	10 (13)
J (23)	Go
3 (26)	
5 (31-2)	K
	K (20-2)
	K (30-7)

What wasn't mentioned was the blunder made by Opponent when he played his Jack. Playing the 5 could have been disastrous as well, if Dealer held 4-5-5-10 or 4-5-10-J. But playing the 3 would have forced Dealer to play a second card, and left him no way of pegging nine holes.

This next hand is similar to those we encountered in Tip #46. You need only two holes to win, Dealer needs five.

You	Dealer
J	6 (16)
J (26)	Go
?	

Your last two cards are 2-4 and the cut is a 5. Does it matter which card you play? At first glance, no. Dealer needs five holes, and whichever card you retain will break up any run he hopes to form. However, if you play the 4 and retain the 2, look what can happen as play continues:

You	Dealer
4 (30-1)	6
2 (8)	7 (15-2)
	7 (22-3)

Had you retained the 4, Dealer, whose cards are all higher than 5, could not have scored 15-2, and would have come up short. The chances of Dealer holding 6-7-7 may be slim, but why take any risk when you can guarantee victory?

48

Look for an Edge
When a Toss Seems 50/50

It's always irritating, when you get a cut that improves your hand, to realize that the same cut fits nicely with the cards you tossed into Opponent's crib. For instance, holding 4-6-7-7-8-J, you save the 6-7-7-8. You aren't displeased when an Ace is cut, as it gives you four more points. Then you remember that you tossed 4-J. On a bad day, Dealer tossed the same cards you did, and the cut increased his crib from four points to thirteen (right Jack, of course).

Toward the end of a game there are times when your discarding decision might hinge on whether or not a cut that will help your hand will also help the crib. Suppose you need 12 holes to win, and Dealer needs 17. Your hand is A-2-6-6-6-K. Should you toss A-K or 2-K? It seems like a tossup. What's the difference?

The difference may lie in Opponent's crib. If you throw the A-K, you'll probably cut a 4. The cribbage gods take great pleasure in annoying you that way. Likewise, when you toss 2-K to the Dealer, you always seem to cut a 3.

But on this particular hand, you *want* to cut a 3. It's one of the cuts that will put you out. So you should toss 2-K. The cut that helps your Opponent's crib as much as any other (as far as you know), puts you out before he gets to count it. And a cut that doesn't help your hand (a 4, for instance), is also less likely to help his crib, so if you don't go out, maybe he won't either.

Now let's look at the same cards, but with a slightly different position. This time you need 17 points to win, and Dealer needs 15. Do you toss A-K or 2-K?

This time you may lose the game even if you get a cut. If you get a cut for a dozen, but peg fewer than five holes, you'll have to hope you can peg out next hand. Of course there may not *be* a next hand, which is why you should now toss A-K. If you don't get a cut for a dozen, you'll have little chance of winning, and it won't matter what you tossed. But if you do get a cut (a 3, in particular), you want Opponent's crib to be empty so that the game goes on, and you peg out next hand. So give him the cards that don't work as well with a 3 cut: the A-K.

To summarize, if a certain cut puts you out, you can afford to toss Opponent cards which are helped by that same cut. When you need a certain cut to have any chance of winning, but that cut *doesn't quite put you out*, toss Opponent cards that *won't* be helped by that cut.

49

If You Guess Opponent's Hand Early, Better Guess All of It

We've seen how important it is to watch your opponent's cards during the play of the hand. After seeing three of her cards, you make an educated guess about her fourth card. If you guess correctly, you sometimes save a couple of holes. As an example, examine these two hands (in each case, you hold 2-4-J-K):

A		**B**	
Opponent	**You**	**Opponent**	**You**
8	J (18)	8	J (18)
8 (26)	2 (28)	8 (26)	2 (28)
2 (30-3)	?	3 (31-2)	?

In Hand A you would next play the 4, not the King. It appears Opponent's last card might be a 5; if it is, she pegs two fewer holes if you play the 4. In Hand B, you would play the King, not the 4. It appears Opponent's last card might be a 4; if it is, she pegs two fewer holes if you play the King.

Often this strategy may be employed after seeing only two of Opponent's cards. If you've seen a 9 and a 4, you might guess that you'll soon be seeing a 2. If you've seen a Queen and a 4, Opponent may well have an Ace. But correctly guessing the general makeup of Opponent's hand does you no good if you fail to make proper use of the information. If you're going to guess Opponent's hand, make sure you guess *all* of it. Situations similar to those that follow arise frequently.

1. You hold 2-6-7-8. The play proceeds:

You	Dealer
8	7 (15-2)
6 (21-3)	9 (30-5)
?	

It appears Dealer might have an 8. So you decide to play your 2 rather than your 7. But is this a smart play? Let's find out. You play the 2, and Dealer plays an 8! He *did* have an 8! You guessed right. Unfortunately, when you play your 7 on his 8 he scores a three-card run with his 6 (or 9). You'd have been better off giving up the 15-2 and breaking up the run with your 2.

2. You hold 4-10-10-J. The play:

You	Dealer
10	5 (15-2)
10 (25)	6 (31-2)
?	

It appears Dealer might have a 4 or a 7. The 7 wouldn't bother you, but you don't want to play a 4 if he has a 4. Or *do* you? You do if he has *two* 4's. Playing the Jack could prove costly.

It's better to give up two points now than three (or more) points later. If it later turns out you wouldn't have given up three points, take heart—it's probably because Opponent's hand isn't as big as it might have been.

50

Remember That Opponent
Can't See Your Hand

You're playing in the final game of a major cribbage tournament. You need four holes to win, while Dealer needs only three. You save 2-3-5-J, the cut is a 5, and you lead the 3. Dealer plays a 4.

You	**Dealer**
3	4 (7)

You can peg three holes now, with either your 2 or your 5. Would you? Of course not. You wouldn't even consider it. You probably wouldn't consider it, even if you had only two points. Dealer *chose* to play a 4 on your 3, instead of something else. Chances are, he's prepared for you to form a run, and will extend the run, winning immediately.

Now let's trade places. You're the dealer. You need three points to win, Opponent has first count. He leads a 3. Your hand is 4-10-J-Q. Your first inclination is to play anything but the 4. Why let him score a three-card run when you get nothing in return? But why should his thought processes be any different than yours were in this situation? It's virtually certain that if you play the 4 on his 3, he's not going to take that run if he can do anything else. He can't see your hand. He doesn't know you're bluffing.

Why try to convince Opponent that you want him to form a run? If you can convince him that you'll win immediately if he plays an Ace, 2, 3, 4, 5, or 6, it's not unreasonable to think he might play a card you can pair. That would put you in the dead hole with a Go yet to come.

In a nutshell, if you play the 10, Jack, or Queen on Opponent's 3, the only way you'll peg is if Opponent plays a 4 (or makes the count 21—unlikely). If you play the 4 on his 3, you peg if Opponent plays a 10, Jack, or Queen.

Convincing Opponent you have the card to extend a run he forms is effective when you threaten to win the game with your counter-pegging. Without that threat, Opponent may take your bait, in the belief that he can "counter-counter-peg," or that it's positionally advantageous to take three points and give up four. When you are close enough to home to peg out, remember, Opponent can't see your hand, and he'll be highly reluctant to play any card that could allow you to win immediately.

Afterword

By now you may be thinking that this is all too much to absorb. Not true! It takes only a minute to play a cribbage hand, and most hands come up over and over. Once you've been faced with the same situations many times, and given them some thought, some of your plays will become automatic. The key is recognizing those situations in which you do need to pause and think things over.

You may also be thinking that if your plays become too automatic, it detracts from your enjoyment of the game. Also not true! You'll probably enjoy the game even more when you start channeling more of your mental energy into situations that warrant it, especially if doing so leads to winning more often. It's satisfying to score up a twenty-four hand, sure, but it can be just as satisfying to success-fully pull off a strategic coup that nets you two measly holes.

Think of the tips in this book as a foundation for suc-cessful play, not as a binding contract. You don't have to adhere to them religiously. Table-feel and intuition can be useful tools as well. I was in the midst of a long series of games online, and had noticed that my opponent never paired my opening lead. Never! At one point I led from a pair of 7's, and he paired. I correctly guessed that he, too, had a second 7, and I resisted tripling. Had he earlier been willing to pair occasionally, I'd have been less wary.

So, don't let the tips in this book tie your hands. Don't rely on them so much that your actions become predictable. Mix up your play. Keep your opponent guess-ing. Fly in the face of all that seems reasonable! But only occasionally.

Index

About the Author

Dan Barlow lives in Durham, NC, with his wife Jennifer, and his son Stephen. Dan won the National Open Cribbage Tournament in 1980. His strategy articles appeared for many years in *Cribbage World*, and many have been collected at the American Cribbage Congress website, www.cribbage.org. His other cribbage books include:

Play Cribbage to Win
Miracles on 4th Street
Cribbage for Experts
Crib Notes
Fun with Cribbage

All are available through The Cribbage Bookstore, online at www.CribbageBooks.com. Dan can sometimes be found playing cribbage at www.Zone.com, pegging under the names Bilbo Peggins and Rufulrabit.

WHAT IS MENSA?

Mensa
The High IQ Society

Mensa is the international society for people with a high IQ. We have more than 100,000 members in over 40 countries worldwide.

The society's aims are:
- to identify and foster human intelligence for the benefit of humanity;
- to encourage research in the nature, characteristics, and uses of intelligence;
- to provide a stimulating intellectual and social environment for its members.

Anyone with an IQ score in the top two percent of the population is eligible to become a member of Mensa—are you the "one in 50" we've been looking for?

Mensa membership offers an excellent range of benefits:
- Networking and social activities nationally and around the world;
- Special Interest Groups (hundreds of chances to pursue your hobbies and interests—from art to zoology!);
- Monthly International Mensa Journal, national magazines, and regional newsletters;
- Local meetings—from game challenges to food and drink;
- National and international weekend gatherings and conferences;
- Intellectually stimulating lectures and seminars;
- Access to the worldwide SIGHT network for travelers and hosts.

See next page for contact information.

For more information about Mensa International:
www.mensa.org
Mensa International
15 The Ivories
6–8 Northampton Street
Islington, London N1 2HY
United Kingdom

For more information about American Mensa:
www.us.mensa.org
Telephone: (800) 66-MENSA
American Mensa Ltd.
1229 Corporate Drive West
Arlington, TX 76006-6103 USA

For more information about British Mensa
(UK and Ireland):
www.mensa.org.uk
Telephone: +44 (0) 1902 772771
E-mail: enquiries@mensa.org.uk
British Mensa Ltd.
St. John's House
St. John's Square
Wolverhampton WV2 4AH
United Kingdom

Acknowledgments
Thanks to Don Lifke of Stat-Help.com, for confirming that the results of my 300-deal tripling experiment (Tip #5) were statistically reasonable. According to Don, one would expect three cards of the same denomination to appear in the top twelve cards of a shuffled deck about 42 percent of the time. That's slightly more often than I came up with experimentally, but close. If it's happening to you a lot more often than that over a long period of time, maybe your deck isn't getting shuffled as well as it should be.

The late Stuart Stromberg's article in the December 1990 issue of *Cribbage Today* inspired Tip #29.

Thanks to Michael Schell, whose website www.Cribbageforum.com inspired Tip #46. Cribbage Forum provides in-depth analysis of cribbage subjects—and links to my own site, www.CribbageBooks.com.

Thanks to my wife Jennifer and my son Stephen, for letting me have extra computer time in order to play thousands of cribbage games, and confirm that the tips in this book actually pay off.